The Abbotsbury Gardens Story

The Abbotsbury Gardens Story

Stephen Griffith

Roving Press

Step-Up Books

© 2015 Stephen Griffith

Published by Roving Press Ltd under the imprint 'Step-Up Books'
4 Southover Cottages, Frampton, Dorset, DT2 9NQ, UK
Tel: +44 (0)1300 321531
www.rovingpress.co.uk

Distributed by Abbotsbury Tourism, West Yard Barn, West Street, Abbotsbury, Dorset, DT3 4JT
Email: info@abbotsbury-tourism.co.uk
Tel: 01305 871130

Every effort has been made to trace the copyright holders, and the author will be happy to correct any mistakes or omissions in future editions.

First published 2015 by Roving Press Ltd

ISBN: 978-1-906651-275

British Library Cataloguing in Publication Data
A catalogue record for this book is available from the British Library

Photographs by Stephen Griffith.

Cover design by Roving Press. Photographs: front – Victorian Garden 1900, Mediterranean Bank; back – Lily Ponds, Cannons at Abbotsbury Castle, Flowering 'Blue Puya' *Puya bertroniana*.

Frontispiece – HRH Prince Charles's visit in 1993, with Head Gardener Stephen Griffith and the Honourable Charlotte Townshend.

Set in 11.5/13 pt by Beamreach (www.beamreachuk.co.uk)
Printed and bound by Henry Ling Ltd, at the Dorset Press, Dorchester, DT1 1HD

Contents

Foreword

According to my notebook account, my first visit to Abbotsbury Subtropical Gardens was in September 1970, though I have a sneaking feeling I made an earlier visit in the 1960s. My notebook entry refers to the Gardens being surrounded by evergreen oak *Quercus ilex*, some of impressive size. Following this brief remark, I get down to the serious business of listing the plants seen, paying particular attention to the less common, the unusual and the impressive. It runs to five pages.

Heading the list is the great Caucasian wingnut *Pterocarya fraxinifolia* (now sadly no more), which stopped me in my tracks. It was a tree of awesome size and spiritual presence. Some years later, I was fortunate enough to see groves of this tree in the river valleys of northern Iran and the Caucasus, but none matching the Abbotsbury tree in its grandeur. My list continued with an eye-popping selection of specials, representing most if not all the countries of the temperate world. A magnificent stand of Chilean myrtle *Luma apiculata*, *Ilex dipyrena* (a noble holly from the eastern Himalaya) and *Notelaea excelsa* (now *Picconia excelsa*) from the famous laurel forests of Madeira and the Canary Islands were enough to convince me that this was no ordinary garden and I knew then that my 'passing visit' would probably take the whole day.

I remember meeting John Hussey, the elderly but helpful Head Gardener, and listening to his stories of earlier days. It was the first of many visits I was to make over the years. In the 1970s I was invited to present a television programme there for BBC South, and then in 1985 when John Kelly was Head Gardener I returned to record another programme, this time for *BBC Gardener's World*. There is no question in my mind, however, that the most significant arrival was that of Stephen Griffith in 1990, who, encouraged by the Ilchester estate and with the help of a close-knit team of gardeners, ushered in a new and exciting era of rescue and revitalisation.

In the 25 years that Stephen has spent here, first as Garden Manager and then Curator and Head Gardener, the Gardens have enjoyed something of a renaissance, with some previously overcrowded if not downright jungly areas robustly yet sensitively cleared to provide new vistas and, with them, opportunities to accommodate new planting or simply more space in which to enjoy what is already established. During this period, the range of new plants established in the Gardens has increased enormously, and for every plant or planting positioned to catch the visitor's eye, there is at least another waiting in the wings to be discovered. It is this mixture of the obvious and the secretive which makes visiting Abbotsbury Subtropical Gardens one of the most rewarding adventures in Britain today.

Roy Lancaster
CBE, OBE, VMH, FI HORT, FLS

Introduction

West Dorset is one of those rural areas where the landscape has remained relatively unchanged with the passage of time. Hill farming and shepherding go on just as described in the novels of Thomas Hardy in the later part of the 19th century. As you take the coast road up out of Abbotsbury village towards Bridport the view across Lyme Bay is breath-taking. Here, hidden in a gently undulating valley just a short distance from the famous Chesil Beach, lies the unique Abbotsbury Subtropical Gardens. Towering evergreen Holm Oaks from the Mediterranean dominate the overhead canopy. Ponds, streams and exotic vegetation from all over the world thrive in its balmy atmosphere, where the shelter and calm serenity are only broken by the shrill cry of Golden Pheasants or the rather startling banter from the call of the resident aviary Kookaburras.

Here lies a very different woodland garden, not trying to conform to trend or design, but letting the plants do the talking. Skilful juxtaposition of bold foliage against upright and linear subtle shades of colour, subduing hot primary colours, this is gardening on the limit of the plants' natural ability to deal with winter cold. Aided by its very own special microclimate, rare and tender exotic plants grow relatively unhindered in the humid sheltered valley in a place where spring comes early and sea frets or misty mornings linger, creating the kind of humidity and warmth more reminiscent of far-off Mediterranean landscapes.

Originally conceived in the 18th century, the Gardens have been held under the stewardship of the Earls and Countesses of Ilchester and their succeeding generations since 1765. There have been wars and changes of sovereignty, successes and neglect, and in this book I hope to tell the Gardens' story, past and present, its influencers and struggles. In trying to unravel the history I discovered all sorts of interesting anecdotes, untold stories and connections with the present owner's ancestors. It is also very much a personnel reflection of the challenges and changes over the years from the point of view of a Head Gardener. A good garden never stands still, and no doubt there will be ever more changes in the future.

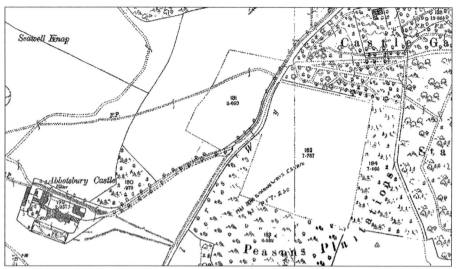

Ordnance Survey map 1902 showing Castle Gardens and Abbotsbury Castle.

Abbotsbury Castle circa 1920.

Abbotsbury Castle Gardens – the Early Days

There is a real sense of history in the landscape around Abbotsbury, from the old buildings to man-made earth movements from days gone by. One cannot help but wonder about the people who once tilled the land, planted trees and laid the first bedding stone to many an ancient stone wall. In order to introduce the reader to the Gardens' story, some text from later in the book has been adapted to bring a sense of historical importance and perspective.

In the 17th century, an ancestor of the present owners of Abbotsbury Gardens, Sir Stephen Fox, was a renowned English politician and paymaster-general to King Charles II. Most importantly, he was the father of the 1st Earl of Ilchester. His home was Redlynch House, Redlynch, in south Somerset.

His son, also named Stephen Fox, became the 1st Baron of Ilchester in 1741, and was raised to the peerage of Lord Ilchester of Ilchester in the county of Somerset. In 1756 he was further honoured when he was made the 1st Earl of Ilchester. Sir Stephen was financial advisor to the Duchess of Buccleuch and it just so happens that one of the oldest Camellias in the garden is called *Camellia japonica* 'Duchess of Buccleuch'. We can only speculate if this planting was a deliberate link, because Sir Stephen died in 1716, many years before the gardens at Abbotsbury were conceived.

The story of the Gardens is also that of the Earls and Countesses of Ilchester, whose family seat became Melbury House at Melbury Sampford near Evershot, which included many acres of fine park, agricultural land and the estate of Abbotsbury 20 miles away on the coast. Although the family title has gone to a kinsman, the present generation and next in line to hold the seat at Melbury continue to manage the estate with great vision and commitment.

The family tree is extensive, with a long and varied history which is interesting in itself. In order to cover some of the more important family history and connections, including horticultural influencers, the family history is given in a chapter near the end of the book.

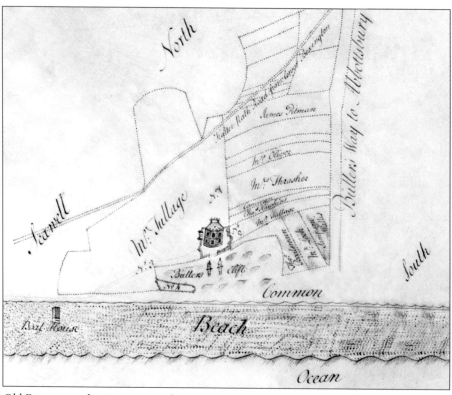

Old Estate map showing gun emplacements at the lookout tower of a fort before Abbotsbury Castle was built in 1765.

In 1758 Elizabeth Fox-Strangways, née Strangways-Horner, inherited the Strangways Estates. Two years previously her husband Stephen Fox had been created the 1st Earl of Ilchester. Sometime around 1765 the first Lady Ilchester built a new house, originally called Strangways Castle; this was built in the 18th-century Gothic Revival style on a bluff above Buller's Clift, close to the shore at a point where Seawell Common adjoined the open fields.

This new 'summer residence' became a more permanent home to Elizabeth after her husband Stephen died in 1776. Lady Susanna Sarah Louisa Fox-Strangways (called Susan), Elizabeth's eldest daughter, recorded in her diary that she assisted her mother's removal to the Castle and helped plan a Rock garden in front of it, sloping down to the sea. The garden had stone arbours at its corners to 'give shelter from whichever quarter the wind might blow'. This garden became renowned in its own right particularly for its collection of *Mesembryanthemums* and early winter- and spring-flowering specimens.

Lady Susanna Fox-Strangways. Painted by Allan Ramsey 1761. (Courtesy of Wikimedia Commons free media.)

Soon after the castle was built another garden was started a quarter of a mile away from it, located in the lee of Peasons Hill within the lower fields of open arable land. It was protected by a wall which enclosed about one and three-quarter acres, and by the early 19th century the site had acquired the name 'Castle Gardens', but the precise layout is unknown. It is most likely that it started as a kitchen garden at around the time the 1st Countess of Ilchester made a more permanent move to the Castle in 1780.

In the 18th century there was something of a renaissance for gardening, with wonderful new plant species being introduced to the country. The excitement of new plant discoveries by intrepid botanists captured the imagination of many keen gardeners. Camellias were beginning to be introduced to Europe in the late 1730s and were the latest fashionable plants to acquire, with their striking large colourful flowers. Some of the older Camellias still growing in the Gardens today are probably from the original introductions from Japan in 1792. Abbotsbury has an ancient grove of these wonderful small trees and many old cultivars grow here: *Camellia japonica* 'Contessa Lavinia Maggi' (raised in 1858), *C. japonica* 'Mathotiana alba' and *Camellia reticulata* 'Captain Rawes' (introduced in 1820); also two very ancient *C. japonica* 'Duchess of Buccleuch'.

Further generations of Fox-Strangways kept the Gardens maintained as a 'pleasure garden' for guests and to indulge their passion for plants. However, on 23 November 1824 a violent storm hit much of the south coast and was referred to as the 'Great Storm'. It was documented in various newspapers and caused quite a sensation at the time. In the book *Elizabeth Lady Holland to her Son* (edited by the 5th Earl of Ilchester) it states that Lord Ilchester 'lost his decoy or Swannery entirely':

The embankment gave way, and the whole is filled with sea and shingles. The house at Abbotsbury was filled with wretched shipwrecked mariners of all nations. Happy for them to meet with shelter and hospitality.

The height of the sea which had been forced over Chesil Beach by the violence of the waves was 22 ft 8 inches above ground at the entrance to the Swannery. It is recorded that '38 pheasants were picked up drowned, besides hares, rabbits, mice, etc innumerable'. There was little reference to the Gardens at this time, presumably because the trees were still quite small in most of the plantations and no mature specimens were there to be blown down. In a letter dated 4 January 1825 from Lady Elizabeth Fielding to William Henry Fox Talbot she says:

On leaving town I went first to Abbotsbury where the late storm has changed the face of nature. The bank of pebbles is greatly lowered and will remain so in future for centuries to come. I saw a boat in the middle of a ploughed field far from the sea. The swans were dispersed far and wide. Fleet church which had stood 500 years was washed away. In the village of Chesil 36 houses were washed away. The sea reached Wyck wood far inland. They are going to erect stones to mark to future generations the points the sea reached. The boathouse at Abbotsbury was the only building on the beach that survived the storm from Weymouth to Sidmouth.

In January 1865 William Fox-Strangways, the 4th Earl of Ilchester, died aged 69, leaving the Abbotsbury Estate to his nephew Henry Edward Fox-Strangways, who thus became the 5th Earl of Ilchester. Although a busy Liberal politician and British Peer, with the influence of his wife Mary he continued in the family tradition of managing the family's Estate and Gardens and adding to the plant collections there.

As villages have changed with the passage of time so do local crafts and industries. Button-making using horn of the local Dorset breed of sheep has long gone, and spar- and hurdle-making is only continued by one or two local craftsmen. However, Abbotsbury village still retains much of its charm and character because of the long-term stewardship of Ilchester Estates and its provision of labour and welfare to locals.

Looking back at the Census of 1880 it is easy to spot familiar local family names that are still in the village and surrounding area:

Emmanuel Vincent	Gardener
Charles Crabb	Garden labourer
William Gill	Groom and gardener
Emma Cribb	Fishing net braider
James Randell	Garden labourer
William Gregary	Game Keeper's assistant
Elizabeth Critchell	Gardener's labourer
William Pittman	General labourer and fisherman
Harry Pittman	Spar maker, hurdler and fisherman
John Dunford	Hurdle maker
James Toms	Walling mason
James Ford	Farmer
John Limm	Carpenter
Alfred Dight	Domestic gardener, Head Gardener
William Trevett	Agricultural labourer

Bill Ferry in bowler hat and crew unloading a haul of mackerel c 1880. Seine netting was carried out by teams working the beach and very often estate staff lent a hand.

The latter part of the 19th century through to the early 20th century has been described as the 'Golden Age' of plant exploration. Joseph Hooker, son of Sir William Hooker (Kew's first public Director with whom William Fox-Strangways was in regular correspondence), had explored the Eastern Himalaya.

Hooker collected 700 species in Nepal and India, adding 25 new species of Rhododendron to the 50 already known and helping create a Rhododendron craze amongst British gardeners. New plant varieties were brought into the country by botanists from Kew Gardens and independently funded nurseries like Veitch of Exeter. There are few West Country gardens that did not house some of their choice plants. Two outstanding trees that still stand in Abbotsbury Gardens which would almost certainly have come from Veitch's nursery are *Quercus* × *hispanica* 'Lucombeana' and the hybrid *Magnolia* × *veitchii* 'Isca' bred by Peter Veitch in 1907 (Isca is the old Roman name for Exeter).

Fol. The Rt Hon. The Earl of Ilchester

EXOTIC NURSERY, King's Road, Chelsea.

Bought of James Veitch Junr.

(SUCCESSOR TO KNIGHT & PERRY)

NURSERY & SEEDSMAN.

1857		£	s	d
June 8th	1 Chorozema Varium nana	-	2	6
	1 " Henchmanni	-	3	6
	1 Dracophyllum gracile	-	2	6
	1 Leschenaultia Formosa	-	2	6
	1 Hoya bella	-	2	6
	1 Bouvardia Longiflora	-	3	6
	1 Eucharis amazonica	-	7	6
	1 Maranta rosea lineata	-	3	6
	1 Justicia Zebrina	-	3	6
	1 Ardisia crenulata Alba	-	3	6
	1 Dieffenbachia Picta	-	5	-
	1 Leschenaultia Biloba Major	-	3	6
	1 Sonerila Margaritacea Gratis	-	-	-
	Basket & packing	-	3	-
		£2	5	6
6th	By Balance of account	1	1	6
		£1	5	-

The Account of the late Earl of Ilchester with James Veitch Jun. was settled up to Jany 23rd 1858 & a receipt given

James Veitch Jn

Invoice for plants from the famous 'Exotic Nursery' of James Veitch Junior, to the Right Honourable Earl of Ilchester, 8th June 1857.

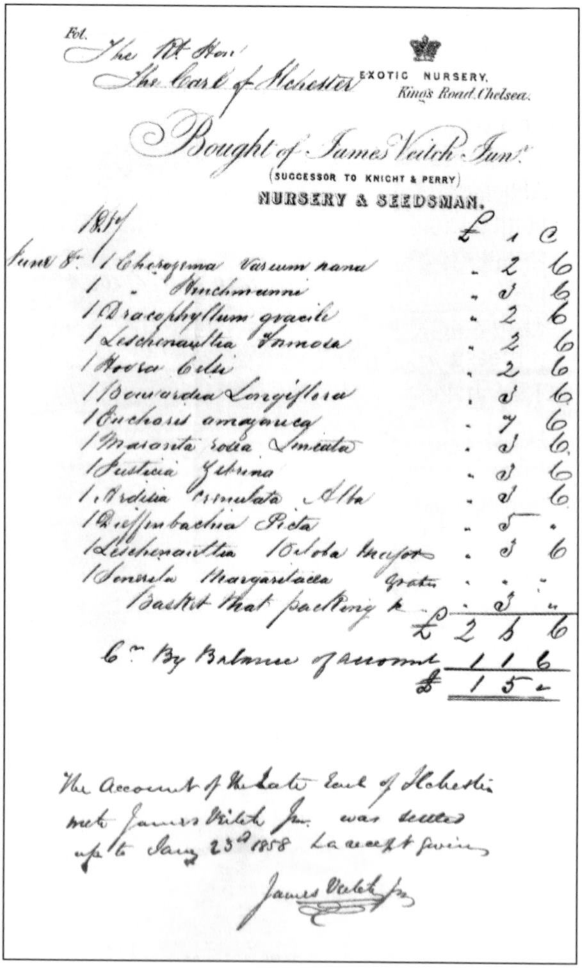

In *The Gardeners' Chronicle* (3 December 1892) Head Gardener Joseph Benbow describes the rockery at Abbotsbury Castle:

> *The rockery, which is close to the sea, is becoming very pretty with the different sorts of* Mesembryanthemums. *They are* M. eckloni, M. barbatum, M. vaginatum, M. tigrinum, M. floribundum *and* M. edule; *the latter I have had sent me from Cannes as cuttings, 3 inches long, and now they measure 4 feet, and are growing permanently outside, as well as a host of other things, such as Sweet Alyssum,* Datura fastuosa, Cytissus, Helianthemum, Auricula, Lithospermum prostratum, Violas, Valottas *and* Calendula. *Her ladyship being delighted with the tout ensemble.*

Unfortunately all the *Mesembryanthemums* were killed during the winter of 1906/7, when –6°C of frost was registered.

Country Life Illustrated (9 December 1899) describes the Gardens with quite a colourful narrative:

> *Abbotsbury is a garden of more than common beauty, a garden of sub-tropical plants, which, in the balmy climate of Dorsetshire, thrive in a manner to arouse envious thoughts in the minds of those placed under less happy conditions.*

The Gardens at that time were an offshoot of the Castle and referred to as the 'Pleasure grounds'. The incredibly sharp and detailed photos taken back in 1899 have been a useful reference to how the Gardens looked then.

Old Abbotsbury Castle seen from the beach.

The year 1899 seems to have had some significance in the importance of the plant collection at Abbotsbury, as *The Gardeners' Chronicle* featured the Gardens that August:

> *Abbotsbury has a proprietor who takes a great interest in outdoor gardening, and especially in completing the adornment of his extensive estate and in experimenting with any and every new plant that can be obtained.*

It is interesting to read that the Gardens were being developed in this quite open yet sheltered valley, being protected in the east by rising land and Holm

Oaks. In addition, each plot was enclosed with reed hurdles and interlaced wattles, which permit some wind to pass through but effectually break the force of the strong gales that sweep up through the valley. The planting of Pampas grass as 'nursery' plants was common. These grassy tussocks helped filter the wind around young trees. Traces of these plants can be seen growing in and around the edges of the shelterbelt plantations today. Apart from the rich and diverse ornamental plant collection, there was once a border 150 yards long planted with grapes; there were some 14 varieties of the new French and American hybrids all trained up iron standards fixed at regular distances 8 ft above the ground and with iron arches.

Once outside the confines of the walled areas, the Gardens had a distinctly wild feel. The *Chronicle* described:

> *Veritable hedges of Bamboos giving such an impression of tropical vegetation as is seldom seen in an English garden.* Bambusa khasyana *were large plants with* Chamaerops fortunei *growing amongst them.*

Bamboos are the largest members of the grass family and some of the fastest growing plants in the world. Specimens were imported directly from Yokohama, Japan, in 1896, and by 1899 Abbotsbury had 40 species. This increased to over 70 different species and cultivars by 2015.

Bamboos growing at Abbotsbury. (From Country Life Illustrated, *1899.)*

> *Rustic steps led up the bank past seedling* Phormium colensoi *and* Phormium tenax. *Here also at the pond sides* Zizania latifolia, *the Japanese Rice. Where the water was shallow were* Richardias [Arum Lilies] *freely planted with* Arundo donax, Papyrus *and Great Gunneras.*

The Dell had running water that wound its way down the valley in a serpentine manner to a pond with a stone rockery dam wall. This is still very much part of the landscape today.

Another source of archive interest is *A Book of English Gardens* by M.R. Gloag (author) and Katharine Montagu Wyatt (illustrator). The latter (1879–1929) was an English landscape painter, architectural painter and water-colourist and she dedicated the chapter on Abbotsbury, which included a water-colour of *Rhododendron falconeri*, to Countess Mary. The book describes the Gardens as being:

Water-colour of Rhododendron falconeri *at Abbotsbury by Katharine Montagu Wyatt from* A Book of English Gardens *(Gloag, 1906).*

… sheltered under a hill which rises between it and the sea, high walls and old Ilex *trees protecting it even further from all cold winds, so successfully is it screened that foreign plants of all kinds will grow and flourish in it, such as Himalayan and Sikkim Rhododendrons, Bamboos, Mimosa, Eucalyptus in thirty varieties, Aloes, Agaves, the New Zealand Laburnum,* Edwardsia Grandiflora, *being a tree of 15 feet high; also the Chile plant* Crinodendron Hookeri. *Every part of the world has been called upon to contribute something to this "Earthly Paradise". Gardening was also much encouraged in the village school.*

The Gardeners' Chronicle (15 February 1913) mentions the Countess as:

A good friend of horticulture, the Dowager Countess of Ilchester has placed all gardeners under a lasting debt of obligation by her generosity in lending the grounds of Holland House for the summer shows of the RHS. She possesses at Abbotsbury a singularly attractive garden, which was described and illustrated in the issue for August 19th, 1899, and the personal interest she takes in horticulture is also evinced by the exhibits of choice plants which she makes frequently at the meetings of the RHS.

On 25 July 1914 the *Chronicle* described:

... a splendid plant of Lagerstroemia indica, *30 ft in height, with pink flowers in August. On one occasion it has borne as many as 200 spikes of bloom. This is doubtless the finest specimen in England. There is also a glorious specimen of* Rhaphitamnus cyanocarpus, *30 ft in height, and 25 ft diameter, which in spring is a dense sheet of blue.* Philadelphus Manteau d'Hermine, *with double white flower was very pretty. Young plants of* Ailanthus vilmoriniana *had leaves 6 ft in length. An uncommon* Pittosporum grandiflorum *was bearing its white-creamy flowers, and the very rare* Villaresia mucronata, *believed to be the only specimen in England, was carrying its white blossoms.* Edwardsia chilensis *and* Laurelia aromatic *were imported directly from Chile in the autumn of 1913.*

The *Laurelia,* now called *Laurelia sempervirens,* still grows in the Victorian Garden and stands at 70 ft tall. Not far away the *Villaresia* has also survived more than 100 years and grown into a Holly-like multi-stemmed small tree. There were a number of plants brought from China by the legendary botanist Ernest Wilson, among which were *Lonicera maackii,* the original of which still grows at Abbotsbury with a gnarled woody trunk in a dense shady corner.

Abbotsbury Castle after the fire in February 1913.

Tragically, on 7 February 1913 a fire started at the Castle with a 'mis-used' candle and the house was burnt to the ground. It was rebuilt in 1915, then demolished sometime in the early 1930s due to excessive damp. The story goes that the builders used beach sand in the cement. The man responsible for the demolition was builder Lewy Basso from Weymouth. Much of the stone rubble was used to make hard-core for the new coastal road section leading up the steep Abbotsbury hill.

The Gardens circa
1898.
Above: Bog garden;
left: Top pond;
right: Monkey
puzzle tree;
below: Yuccas.

The Local War Effort

World War I and II were obviously disruptive times for village life, marked with the sad loss of many young men who went to fight. They also manifested themselves in a general decline in non-essential working practices. The reduced labour force meant that many estates around the country suffered, including Abbotsbury. Food rationing and coupons were initiated by the Ministry of Food, and later, owing to the fuel shortage, a Household Fuel and Lighting Order came into operation in August 1918. A drastic reduction in coal consumption was imposed, which led to only essential supplies being issued. In practice, this would have halted the use of heated stove houses for keeping ornamental plants.

A sinister threat lurking just off the coast, immediately below the Gardens, was German submarines. On New Year's Day morning 1915, *HMS Formidable*, a pre-dreadnought battleship, was struck by torpedo and sank a few miles south west of Portland with over 790 men on board. Captain Loxley went down with his ship and was seen by a survivor standing on the bridge until the last minute with his faithful companion Bruce, an Airedale Terrier. The dog's body was washed up on the beach at Abbotsbury and buried in the Gardens, commemorated with a headstone. The story made world news and even a book (*Captain Loxley's Little Dog*, Hodder and Stoughton, 1915). The Ship's chaplain and former curate of nearby Burton Bradstock Rev G. Brooke Robinson was also lost.

Captain Loxley.

Because of incidents like this the renowned Bridport net industry started to take a different direction, with anti-submarine nets being produced by Messrs W. Edwards and Son. An airship hanger was established at Powerstock, from where they launched aerial patrols all along the coast searching for the dark shadows of submarines.

Head Gardener Joseph Benbow had the sad news that his son Captain Edwin Louis Benbow MC, 85th Squadron Royal Air Force, was killed in action near Ypres on 30 May 1918 aged 22. He is buried in St Nicholas churchyard, Abbotsbury, and commemorated on a brass plaque in the church.

Around 1940 German invasion looked imminent. The Dorset coastline was suspected as being a potential landing area for the German 6th Army, under codename 'Operation Sea Lion', and its defence came under the responsibility of the United States of America V Corps. Abbotsbury and particularly Chesil Beach, along with Studland Bay in Purbeck, were considered to be the most vulnerable areas in the south west for a German landing. In charge of the Abbotsbury defences in July 1940 was the 6th Bn Durham Light Infantry. By December 1940 the Abbotsbury sector was held by the 8th Bn Essex Regiment which held a series of beach-front localities. For all-round defence they had automatic weapons, such as the Vickers medium machine guns and Lewis guns sighted on fixed lines to fire along the beach and from pillboxes constructed at 500-yard intervals. Behind the

Local Home Guard 1940. Back row: A. Huddy, T. Price, W. Limm, L. Toms, M. Ford, S. Spicer, G. Horlock, A. Hayne. Centre row: J. Churchill, E. Bartlett, G. Gill, W. Arnold, W. Roper, G. Ford, T. Horlock. Front row: W. Ford, R. Joyce, C. Hutchings, S. Price, A. Lewington, G. Gill, W. Dunford.

front line troops, the village was organised and defended locally by both Weymouth and Dorchester Battalions of the Dorset Home Guard, who had several serving members who were staff at Abbotsbury Gardens.

Behind the infantry beach-front defences, artillery was positioned on the hills to the rear and at the back of the Gardens. On the hillside just below the Gardens ('Jurassic View Point') there is a circular Norcon pillbox where 4-inch gun emplacements of the Abbotsbury Battery once stood. A further gun position for a 6-pounder was built on the old Abbotsbury Castle site and a 25-pounder Field Artillery Battery was also in support. A massive double row of concrete cubes was constructed where Chesil Beach joined the Fleet Lagoon, its purpose to stop German armour gaining access. These still stand across the beach and are known as the 'Tank Teeth'. An anti-tank ditch was dug along the back of the beach, backed up by tubular-steel scaffolding known as 'Z.I. Obstacle' which ran along the head of the beach as far as the lagoon. Further to the rear, extensive minefields were laid.

'Tank Teeth' on the beach.

Microclimate, Topography and Geology

What makes Abbotsbury different to many other gardens in the UK is its microclimate. A combination of geographical factors have helped to provide an almost 'Mediterranean' environment, with long dry summers and wet mild winters, but without the extreme summer heat. In simple horticultural terms, the Gardens can grow a wide range of more tender plants outside, without the protection of a greenhouse. This can clearly be seen by the range of plants growing from all over the world in what is generally a cool temperate climate.

The main reason the Gardens are so mild is their proximity to the sea. Aided by the Gulf Stream the sea heats up over summer and this heat is partly retained over winter, warming the land by as much as 2–3°C. Average winter minimum temperatures in the Gardens are –3 to +3°C and annual precipitation is 750 mm. Occasionally we have experienced temperatures as low as –7°C (for short periods) during the coldest part of a winter, so even Abbotsbury has to wrap up and protect soft-growing plants sometimes.

Protecting plants from the worst of winter.

Other gardens around the western coastline of the British Isles also have a mild microclimate that relies heavily on the Gulf Stream or its northern extension, the North Atlantic Drift. This is one of the strongest ocean currents in the world. The Gulf Stream moves warm water from the Gulf of Mexico north into the Atlantic. Some scientists say the powerful ocean current that bathes Britain and northern Europe in warm waters from the tropics is weakening dramatically, a consequence of global warming. Unchecked, they fear it will trigger more severe winters and cooler summers across the region.

The unusually hard winter of 2011.

The Gardens are essentially situated in a woodland valley, which somewhat protects them from the salt-laden sea gales in winter. There is less possibility of advection frost, which is more associated with large-scale incursions of cold air with a well-mixed, windy atmosphere and temperature that is often sub-zero, even during daytime. However, the Gardens are prone to 'frost hollow formation', where cold air runs downhill and collects to form cold spots. Local vegetation has an important part to play in reducing frosts here. Despite the 1990 storms there are still many Holm Oaks (*Quercus ilex*), which are evergreen trees that retain their leaves in winter. They act like a giant blanket, helping to reduce radiation frost,

Pond and Tree Ferns in winter.

which can cause damage to plants. The tree canopy blocks outgoing long-wave radiation and reflects it back down to the ground, storing energy to help keep temperatures up.

The second geographical benefit is the local topography. Originally, alternating layers of sands, clays and limestone were laid down, the latter under shallow tropical seas. Millions of years later, Alpine Orogeny caused the formation of folded rocks that pushed upwards. These gradually eroded, leaving a long chalk escarpment and ridgeway that runs a couple of miles behind the Gardens. This creates the 'rain-shadow effect' over the Gardens. Warm moist south-westerly winds are brought in over the sea. Air is forced up over the ridge, causing cooling, followed by condensation and cloud formation. It can be raining in Dorchester all day (only 10 miles inland) whilst Abbotsbury is in glorious sunshine. The rain-shadow effect also means that we are blessed with more average hours of sunshine than other parts of Dorset, which in turn gives a longer growing season. Plants get the chance to harden off their soft growth in time for the coming winter, which in effect makes them tougher.

Understanding the local microclimate is an important factor in growing plants in areas that are colder than their natural environment and climatic regions. Rudolph Geiger wrote a very influential and forward-thinking book about microclimatology, *The Climate Near the Ground*, which is still regarded as the 'bible' of microclimatology.

The geology of Abbotsbury Gardens is divided. To the north west, use was made of a south-facing bank to create the 'Mediterranean Garden'. Here, Abbotsbury ironstone from the Corallian sequence has 'faulted' against

Kimmeridge Clay, which forms the soil for the rest of the Gardens. The softer clay has been eroded away, leaving the bank exposed with oolitic ironstone, which is where fossilised Brachiopods are often dug up. This ironstone occurs in various other places where erosion has taken place, creating an unusual pocket of acid soil, which is why we can grow Rhododendrons, Camellias, Azaleas and Proteas yet the surrounding limestone country is not suitable for such ericaceous plants.

Brachiopod fossils unearthed in the Mediterranean Garden.

Early Restoration, Development and Set-backs

Lady Teresa Agnew and her first husband Simon Monckton-Arundell, 9th Viscount Galway, started to restore the Gardens in the late 1960s. After two World Wars the Gardens had fallen into decline as the labour force had reduced. Much of the woodland valley and its early 19th-century planting had become engulfed by vegetation, a sea of brambles and scrub. Lady Teresa employed a keen amateur gardener called John Hussey to make the first attempt at clearing the overgrown woodland. He was a sprightly 65-year-old when he first started helping Lady Teresa with a background in the motor industry. Unfortunately his enthusiasm was not matched by knowledge and some of the trees cut down to make a lawn were actually the beautiful summer-flowering *Eucryphia*, of which there is now only one survivor.

After he retired for a second time, John Kelly took over as Head Gardener. John had a background in growing Alpines and was a keen journalist, author and occasional part-time presenter of the BBC's *Gardener's World*. The Gardens were extended by 4 acres and included some new varieties donated from the plant-hunting Sino-British Expedition to Cangshan (SBEC), China, in 1981. However, John's passion was his writing and he left in 1988, leaving the Gardens somewhat in limbo.

Planting plans drawn up by Hilliers and Sons in 1964 were discovered again in the 1990s. Many of the proposed plants are now present, but there is little evidence that the designs were closely implemented. Lady Teresa was passionate about old-fashioned flowering shrub roses and these were planted frequently in her time. However, many have been superseded by the modern repeat-flowering roses of today.

Lady Teresa died in 1989 and her daughter, the Honourable Charlotte Anne Monckton, inherited the Estate. The responsibility to manage and upkeep the Gardens was immense – not only because of its botanical importance but also due to the long unbroken historical ownership by the family since its conception in 1765 by the 1st Countess of Ilchester.

To exacerbate things, on the morning of 14 January 1990 a storm raged

Storm damage in 1990.

along the South West, buffeting headlands, coastal towns and villages. By midday, gusts of 95 mph were ripping limbs from trees and uprooting enormous Oaks, tiles were flying from roof tops, and chimney stacks were disintegrating as bricks fell loose from their columns. The Gardens took the brunt of the storm.

Their first line of defence from the high winds were the ancient Holm Oaks that formed a shelterbelt just a few hundred metres from the beach. However, they were knocked down like skittles, crashing through the wooden perimeter fences and leaving their roots exposed. Fallen trees blocked the only access road to the Gardens and Coast Guard Cottages, and all power and telephone lines were cut. The weather showed no respect to the rare and choice trees and by evening the damage tally had risen to over 100 specimens. As well as the physical damage, the storm severely affected the Gardens' vital shelter, so important for protecting the plant collections.

Fallen Holm Oaks after the storm in January 1990.

The Gardens had become rather drab, run down and overgrown and the devastating storm damage just added to the need for change. The Head Gardener position was revisited and the job spec called for detailed plans to halt the decline. Infrastructure was to be reviewed, the plant collections were to be enhanced, and business and tourism were to be developed. Commercial acumen was essential to run the new plant centre. The owners and trustees required a 10-year plan. No one expected an overnight success and after the storm damage it took nearly a year of timber hauling and root removal, followed by remedial tree surgery, just to establish a baseline. The Gardens were mostly dark overgrown woodland with little or no ground-cover plants.

Very few choice and rare shrubs had survived and the *Camellia japonica* cultivars seemed to dominate. The few interesting specimens included *Osmanthus yunnanensis, Cornus × ormonde* and a huge oak-like variety of the rare 'False Olive' *Picconia excelsa,* an evergreen tree endemic to Macronesia. But these had at least partially succumbed to storm damage and then Honey fungus in the early 1990s. Advancing underground root systems of the vigorous 'Square-stemmed Bamboo' *Chimonobambusa quadrangularis* had swallowed up Hydrangeas that once grew in vast drifts.

Great bows from the *Rhododendron arboreum* hybrids had snapped or fallen, some forming naturally layered shrubberies. One discovery was a tall trunk from a tree fighting its way through scrub to reach daylight. On closer inspection its large glossy and serrated leaves turned out to be a giant Holly *Ilex fargesii* ssp *fargesii,* a native of the mountain slopes of Sichuan, China.

It had the feel of a 'lost romantic garden' but lacked a sense of order. Paths led nowhere in particular and a lack of pruning made it feel hemmed in. Vistas and peep holes were needed to catch the eye and entice the visitor through the Gardens.

When I took over as Head Gardener in 1990, staffing levels were at their highest since I have worked here, with seven gardeners, yet the garden looked uncared for and run down. This was through no fault of the staff but due to the lack of direction. Months were spent simply pulling brambles, clearing paths and pruning. At just 33 years old I was the 'new kid on the block' and I had to win over the staff and the Gardens.

February 1991 saw weeks of freezing cold weather with blizzards across the country. Abbotsbury didn't escape and it became apparent that even usually mild West Dorset could get pretty cold in winter. Returning from a Management Training Course, I found ponds frozen over and some very sad-looking Palms, tender perennials and blackened fleshy leaves of Aloes.

The Agaves had fared better. So much for the microclimate! I later learnt that although temperatures here went down to –7°C, some parts of the country had seen –14°C, so perhaps we had got away lightly. In fact, after a decade of generally mild winters there was complacency, with tender plants being left outside all year. Colder winters were back with a vengeance, it seemed.

Unfortunately, in the Castle fire of 1913 many documents and interesting archives associated with the Gardens were lost. However, in 1991 a small green book was unearthed from an office drawer at the Gardens. It was the *Abbotsbury Gardens Catalogue of Plants*, containing a listing of over 4,000 plants growing here in 1899. This was a vital piece of historic information, providing an invaluable insight. Many plant names have changed since the catalogue was printed, but it is easy enough to check up on old pseudonyms. Even country names have changed, as the book refers to plants coming from places like New Holland, Ceylon and Mesopotamia.

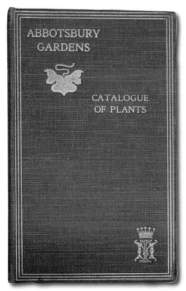

Abbotsbury Gardens Catalogue of Plants, *1899. On the cover is a crown over the ornate letters 'MI'; the book was privately printed by Hatchards, 187 Piccadilly, London, for Lady Mary, 5th Countess of Ilchester.*

It was becoming clear that in their heyday the Gardens had a very important plant collection, and that many plants had died off or been smothered by weeds over the years, as well as suffering neglect from lack of a labour force during the two World Wars.

Mr Hussey revisited the Gardens in 1992. He was in his eighties and used a walking stick but proudly pointed out all the work they had achieved during his time as Head Gardener in clearing parts of the woodland, constructing concrete steps and introducing pathways.

The Ten-Year Plan

To restore this maritime, subtropical, woodland, valley garden needed careful planning. A balance needed to be achieved, with new development overlaying the historical 18th- and 19th-century background, content and landscape. Knowing where to start would be key.

Old, tired and starved shrubberies, areas of dry soil and no ground cover, overgrown thickets and pruning work everywhere were a constant concern. The gardeners were stretched to maintain the entire garden and it was like 'spinning plates', just keeping it going as more was added, and always in a slight panic. Short-term plans were formulated and notes were made of potential future improvements, but progress was slow. A coherent ten-year plan was needed.

All ideas were captured in work schedules and ordered by importance. Jobs included looking at all the old borders, tired shrubberies and pathways and planning future 'vistas', repairing leaking ponds, restoring silt traps, building a children's play area, extending the car park, building a new perimeter fence, and phasing in new buildings like the restaurant, ticket office and shop.

Restoring tired borders and old shrubberies.

As the Gardens began to develop apace, we tried to some extent to follow the style of a botanical garden by providing, where possible, the native growing conditions for each new plant accession. This meant developing geographical areas within the garden; thus we had the 'Sino-Himalayan Glade' for plants from Asia, the 'Southern Hemisphere gardens' for Australia and New Zealand, a 'Mediterranean Bank' and a 'Chilean collection'. Of course time stands still for no man, and in no time at all we had completed

Construction of the Old Colonial Restaurant, 1997.

Family-friendly events in the Gardens.

most of the ten-year works. We were now moving forward as the Gardens entered another phase, that of a venue for events and entertainment, bringing in another audience.

In 1998 Mrs Townshend brought an important guest along to one of the quarterly garden meetings, Sir Simon Hornby, newly elected President of the Royal Horticultural Society. He was immediately taken by the Gardens and felt more must be done to continue the good restoration work and highlight the Gardens' uniqueness. He was a tall man in stature and had an enthusiastic, forceful, yet persuasive way about him, always complimentary and encouraging. He would put us in contact with other horticultural professionals who we could bounce ideas off and look to for support. A month later we had a meeting with John Bond, Keeper of the Royal Gardens at Windsor Great Park. He agreed to act as a consultant and visit Abbotsbury every three months to view progress. His plant knowledge and ideas on managing woodland gardens were of immense value.

Sadly, John Bond died in 2002, and he was replaced later that year by Martin Lane Fox. He is a renowned garden designer and was also the Vice President to the Royal Horticultural Society. Martin's influence was more with the structural features and classical lines that have brought another dimension to the Gardens. Martin retired in 2013, but we were fortunate to add the distinguished Roy Lancaster to our panel. His knowledge and enthusiasm never

John Houston, Abbotsbury Tourism General Manager (left), with distinguished author, plantsman and garden consultant Roy Lancaster.

dwindles. Roy has had a long association with Abbotsbury over the years and has kindly provided many rare plants that are now well established and adding interest to the woodland flora.

Restoration from 1990

Where do you start when restoring a garden of this scale that is in need of tender loving care at all levels? There were three important considerations: (1) management of the special microclimate, as we had to maintain the balance of shelter, tree canopy and humidity; (2) development of the plant collection to harmonise with the charm and natural setting of the woodland valley; and (3) maintenance of the historical importance of the site and the need to strike a balance between tourism and income, on the one hand, and retaining the Gardens' semi-wild character, clear of commercial clutter, on the other.

Following the 1990 storm many of the mixed shingle paths had become rutted with craters after the huge Holm Oaks were uprooted. The stone edges had all but disappeared through neglect and the passage of time. They had to be raised and new rocks added to the path edge. Whilst repairing paths we uncovered original layers of path material set down in the 1800s. A letter dated 23 December 1851 from a Mr Medlycott of Sherborne to Lord Ilchester reveals the process of their construction:

My Dear Lord Ilchester,

*   After the winter season is passed I shall be able to give you a better report of my gravel walks. Still, I may say, they have born the frost well, and have been in no way injured. The walks have been formed and rolled smoothly with common gravel or sand or even coal ashes. They were then covered with gas tar poured from a water pot in hot weather, or prepared over a small fire (to keep it liquid) and then covered with prepared sifted gravel sufficiently thick to cover the tar, and rolled down at once. A little quick lime also mixed with the undercoat of gravel or sand will also make it bind firmer. There should also be a drain on each side of the walks, which should be formed, for the wet to run off it. I have often advised the desirability of the garden walks and school ground of Burton Hospital, which are made of quick lime, coal ashes and gas tar. I have no weeds to contend with and the walks have been far dryer than the ordinary gravel walks. The gas tar you could pursue from Yeovil and I would advise you're giving early notice of it as it is much in demand, I would certainly advise you not to attempt it until the wet season is over.*

Many paths had originally been topped off with Chesil Beach shingle. Commercial extraction in the last century is said to have removed 1.1 million tonnes from the beach between Abbotsbury and West Bay. Any removal of pebbles is now totally banned in order to assist in the long-term survival of the beach. The shingle pebbles were also used to surround the clay pipes in the drainage ditches. During World War II, soldiers billeted in the Gardens used the pebbles in concrete mixes for defence walls and hard-standing areas for the mizzen huts. In 1940, Army sappers constructed concrete roads down to the beach, to provide access for military vehicles, and incorporated beach pebbles in the mix.

Rebuilding paths near the West Gate, 1991.

Along the perimeter of the Gardens next to the road that leads to the beach was an attractive redwood shiplap panelled fence. This fence was unfortunately destroyed as mighty Holm Oaks crashed through it in the 1990 storm. The roadside gaps in the fence had created access to the Gardens for Roe deer, which quickly became a major garden pest at the time. A new electrified deer fence was constructed, which had two lines of wire about 1.5 m above the lower section of meshed rabbit fence wire. Unfortunately startled deer could leap right through the wires without any shock at all if all their feet were off the ground at the same time. Also, as the Gardens were regaining their popularity, a number of unsuspecting tourists had complained of receiving a shock, and although it was safe the electricity was removed.

The fence had made the Woodland Valley reasonably secure from deer, but there was still a healthy rabbit population that had to be reduced. They tended to sit under the cover of thickets, scrubland and fallen branches during the day. There were no rabbit warrens or underground tunnels to send in ferrets or where we could use purse nets, so we resorted to evening or early morning soirées with a Labrador and shotgun.

The walls of the Walled Garden stand testament to the skills of their original builders, using only lime mortar to bond the stonework. The wall still has many old hand-forged nails sticking out of the mortar, indicating that an abundance of climbers plus fan-trained and cordoned fruit were once grown here. The *Gardens Catalogue* of 1889 lists 27 cultivars of apple, 25 pear, 18 plums and 2 apricots.

When we looked in detail, many of the paths were simply buried from years of leaf litter accumulation. The original stone edges were unearthed and only needed lifting and resitting with a fresh layer of self-binding path gravel. The corners of the Walled Garden were so dark and hidden by tall trees and shrubs that it was like walking into a dark cave. Many of these plants were the original Camellias, some reaching 8–9 m tall yet only producing small flowers. They had not been pruned and had outgrown the site, in scale and proportion. We lacked experience in pruning Camellias of this size, but our tree surgery skills were employed by precision chain-sawing large limbs back to new growing points and reducing leading shoots by almost 50 percent. This gave a radical new look to the Walled Garden and suddenly let much more light in to the struggling lower plant cover. The Camellia trees looked quite bare and stumped and we were concerned about going too far, but it turned out to be a great success. The pruned trunks developed new shoots by the end of the first summer, then flower buds in the second year.

By unlocking the entangled climbers and shrubs we unveiled the tall Chusan Palms (*Trachycarpus fortunei*). They followed the line of the west-facing wall and led to a 'bricked in' section of the Walled Garden, where once there would have been a doorway and quite possibly the path that led down the road to the Castle.

Beach Farm, as it was known, is situated just off the road that leads to the beach, adjacent to the southern end of the Gardens. In 1989 Ilchester Estates converted the outbuildings there into a large workshop and storage area. One half of the building was for the Estate's maintenance department, the other became the Gardens' nursery and machinery workshop. Hard-standing areas were constructed to house polytunnels and a greenhouse. From here we started to produce plants for sale at the Plant Centre and Shop.

The bulk of the Gardens sits in the shelter of a mild and moist woodland valley, and many of the original Oak and Ash trees that were planted to form

Stavordale Wood in the early 1800s were now well over 45 m tall. They were beginning to look a little precarious, shedding large limbs of dead wood, and several had large cavities at the base of the trunk. The decision was made to fell one or two of the ancient specimens. The biggest Ash tree in the garden was totally hollow and oozed sap down the trunk, with signs of the Honey Fungus *Armillaria armillaria (mellea)* (tell-tale orange mushrooms). Tree surgeons were brought in, and because it was so big and top heavy we decided to 'direct fell' it out through the perimeter fence and into the surrounding woodland, using a tractor and winch. After precision hinge cuts and hammering in metal wedges, the giant tree began to fall in slow motion, then twisted at the last moment due to its hollow trunk.

At one time the Gardens had no less than four 'Champion trees' on the Tree Register for Great Britain and Northern Ireland. The very tall 'Tulip tree' *Liriodendron tulipifera*, at well over 40 m, was looking very weak and supporting itself by growing through an enormous nearby Wingnut (*Pterocarya fraxinifolia*) tree. There was no point in keeping it just for the record book if it didn't contribute to the balance of the surrounding tree canopy, so it was felled in 1996. This made it lighter for the understory shrub planting. Other felling decisions were of course forced on us by nature. Again, at over 40 m, we probably had the tallest *Rosa* 'Kiftsgate' in the country. It scrambled through a very tall and sparsely needled Scots Pine tree, *Pinus sylvestris*. One hardly noticed it being in flower as it was so high up in the tree canopy. Perversely, it was as if this giant Himalayan rose was supporting the Pine. The trunk of the tree was showing signs of decay and looked like it may not last. It came crashing down in the

Abbotsbury
Sub-Tropical Gardens

Season 1967

These Gardens will be open to the public on

WEEKDAYS   From 24th MARCH until further notice from 10 a.m. to 4.30 p.m.

SUNDAYS   From 26th MARCH until further notice from 2 p.m. to 6 p.m.

ADMISSION: ADULTS 2/- CHILDREN 1/-

THE STRANGWAYS ESTATES LTD.
ESTATE OFFICE, ABBOTSBURY
WEYMOUTH

Opening times and entrance fees for 1967.

storm of 1999, with surprisingly little collateral damage.

In order to boost the business and make it more efficient, a new shop was built in 1990 along with a nursery and plant centre. The family had provided generous subsidies in the past, so dedicated business plans were produced to make the Gardens self-supporting. An old 1967 advert for the Gardens shows the entrance fee of 2 shillings. The new ticket office was to be supported by an improved plant sales area to replace the 'standing out' area underneath the trees.

Old entrance and shop in 1970, now used as an office.

The new shop being built in 1990.

The old nursery and toilets, 1986. Glass houses on the left have been replaced by the Colonial Restaurant.

The centre of the Victorian Garden had some old-fashioned shrub roses in it that only flowered for a couple of weeks a year and were very old and woody. In order to bring more seasonal interest to this part of the garden we decided to give the central island bed a spring planting scheme with bulbs, following through with a more typical Victorian Subtropical bedding scheme, using tender perennials and glass-house plants planted outside for the summer. This technique is often known as 'plunge bedding'. This is the first area that visitors walk through, and we wanted this bed to catch the eye and entice the visitor through towards the West Lawn.

Wear and tear from visitors' feet on the lawn had always been a problem so we introduced a stone slab path to take away the necessity of resowing grass each year. Car parking also became an issue every year, as cars would get stuck on the wet grass, and muddy areas soon became large holes. In 1993 we extended the car park into the surrounding field and laid a hard-surface access road. Trees and shrubs were chosen that were wind and salt tolerant and some that would eventually form shade for cars to park under.

The Sunken Lawn area is set down in a small hollow within the Walled Garden, overlooked from the Tea Garden above. The dominant Chusan Palms that grow in the lawn are quite possibly the tallest in the UK. Planted around 1895, they really add an air of the subtropics, although their crown of palm fronds is thinning, reminiscent of a bad hair day. They have been so successful that they self-seed and produce germinating seedlings that crop up all over the garden. However, the problem with Palms growing in the lawn is that they create a natural obstacle for the lawn mower.

The Sunken Lawn, 1899. (Courtesy of Country Life.*)*

The Sunken Lawn today.

To improve the line of sight and create a more formal Continental scene we introduced a series of circular paved areas to surround the base of the Palms. To complete the scene we used large terracotta pots and pithoi, handmade in Crete. Large clay olive jars also help create the feel of a Moorish Spanish courtyard.

Interesting Discoveries

A culvert with a natural stream runs directly under the road and into the Gardens, feeding storm and spring water from the hills behind. Since the Walled Gardens' conception in 1765, a short section of this stream has been covered over with large stone slabs and earth. It was possible to hear water flowing underground but not to see it. In order to make a feature of this running water we decided to unearth the culvert to expose the watercourse and open up the streamside.

After digging down a couple of metres we found the stone slabs that had been used to cover the stream, but most of the dry-stone worked walls had crumbled and been dislodged and entangled by the Wingnut trees' root systems. By collecting stones from a disused perimeter wall in the Gardens we

Culverted stream uncovered.

soon had enough material to rebuild the support walls of the earthen banks of the culvert. We found a pair of the large stone slabs, which we used to make a footbridge across the stream. This was completed in 1997. Whilst digging out some of the earth spoils and silt, one of the gardeners came across a fragment of ancient pottery. It had scored wavy lines of decoration over the chestnut-brown clay that had once been baked hard in some Iron Age furnace (as identified by an archaeologist).

Today, when one views the charming brook that flows through the Walled Garden near the Bothy you could easily assume that the fern-covered walls and quaint little footbridge had been there for centuries.

The culvert in 2013 looking very natural with self-sown ferns.

Back in 1993, at the bottom of the Sunken Lawn near the base of the Wingnut tree we made another discovery. A large rectangular slab of grey slate lay on the ground, half covered in ivy. It took four men to lift it and as it upended we found it had been hiding the top of a stone-lined well that still had a good head of water in it. The slate slab turned out to be the base section for a rectangular trough. It was originally a sort of reservoir to hold water pumped from the well. The well itself was just a hole in the ground so we built up the stonework to create a rustic well head. I found an unusual carved pottery head, which we cemented into the stonework and within a couple of years it was beginning to look like one of the original landscape features. Later we added an ornate cast-iron hand pump.

Whilst digging or weeding in the Gardens we have unearthed many of the original cast metal plant labels, which look as clear to read as when they were cast over a hundred years ago. Sometimes we find the even older lead labels that were often used as dispatch labels that came in attached to plants from nurseries.

The overgrown shrubbery had layers of Rhododendron and Ivy;

Old metal plant labels once used in the Gardens.

under it we discovered an old sword lying in the decaying leaves. It was rusted through and the wooden handle had long since rotted away, yet it was exciting to find this historic piece of armoury. Still in its scabbard, the sword brought to mind images of piracy and smuggling. An expert's opinion later suggested it might be a cavalry sabre or, due to its small size, a short dress sword from the early 19th century. Of course, someone may have been using it as a garden scythe.

Deep inside the woodland garden the path meanders up through the 'Secret Walk', with its fine collection of Asiatic trees and shrubs. Hidden in the undergrowth under layers of fallen Rhododendron it is possible to make out deep ridges or terraces known as strip lynchets. They were hand dug or ploughed into the hillside to create level strips for crop production in Celtic field systems.

In another area of the Woodland Valley, where the stream trickles through and over a large rock, we unearthed a stone wall that was almost completely covered with silt. On closer inspection we could see that this was

Rusty sword found in the overgrown shrubbery.

once the edging for a small pond. The only way to find out was to dig down and remove several tons of earth, a slow process with spade, shovel and wheelbarrow, but eventually we found a cement floor, along with a recess in the stonework for some sort of gate. This turned out to be a Victorian silt trap, designed to prevent the sediment brought down from the hills contaminating the larger ponds.

In 1765 when Elizabeth, Countess of Ilchester, made plans to build her summer residence overlooking Chesil Beach, she chose the site of an existing stronghold or watch tower that was possibly built to guard the coast when

The old ships' cannons raised from Lyme Bay were originally put on display below Abbotsbury Castle.

the French had ambitions to invade in 1759. The French were thwarted by the British Royal Naval blockade. The old Estate map of 1765 (see page 4) depicts cannons facing out to sea and two 4- to 6-pounders still exist in the Gardens. One cannon has been identified as French with roman numerals added, indicating it was a captured gun. The Great Storm of 1824 lifted the shingle on the beach beneath the old Castle and exposed five more cannons; these are likely to have been naval armament for a Brig-sloop, possibly made for the East India Company between 1770 and 1820. Many of these cannons have been resited at the Jurassic View Point on the hill to the south of the Gardens, where they once again face the sea.

Tree Surgery and Woodland Management

In January 1990 one of the biggest storms to hit Dorset that century blew in and pounded the Gardens. Many fine and ancient trees were uprooted and blown over. After the significant clean up, the Gardens took on a more open feel. Despite the generally catastrophic damage, overall it became apparent that the Gardens had benefited from the storm. 'You can't see the wood for the trees' was a saying that certainly rang true here, as many vistas and viewpoints had been lost due to neglect over the years.

After a professional tree inspection, a list was drawn up of those requiring dead wood and branch removal, crown reduction, thinning and, if necessary, felling. We had tree surgery experience, so a considerable amount of the more cosmetic dead wooding and crown thinning was done in-house. However, this took our focus off our core responsibilities and priorities, so contract tree surgeons were brought in, which also quickened the pace. Our gardeners' chainsaw skills improved after further training, and the occasional by-product was some cleverly crafted garden seats.

Tree surgery is an ongoing process in the Gardens.

Where larger timber appeared sound, with no rot, a contractor was used who set up a double-ended Trekka saw. This is a two-man operation that can cut out large timber planking on the spot, the Gardens being too densely

Creating planks with a two-man Trekka saw.

planted to be able to bring in heavy timber-hauling machinery. This proved a cost-effective use of home-grown timber that could be stored and seasoned, then sold on to carpentry or craft workshops.

Ancient trees, a mix of Holm Oak (*Quercus ilex*), Common Oak (*Quercus robur*) and Ash (*Fraxinus excelsior*), had dominated the overhead canopy and helped create the unique microclimate. Not all were lost in the storm, but it became a major consideration to plug the gaps to maintain the existing trees in order to keep the harmony and balance of this mild garden. Pathways and open spaces became lighter and this helped the understory shrubs and groundcover plants to thrive.

Around this time the government introduced 'set aside' subsidies to encourage arable land to be taken out of production. This provided an opportunity to plant new shelter trees on the Estate's surrounding farmland. This was undertaken by Andy Poore, Ilchester Estates forestry manager, who had been involved in similar projects across the South West and nationally. The work was also partly funded by English Heritage 'Storm Damage' grants.

A really remarkable giant Caucasian Wingnut tree (*Pterocarya fraxinifolia*) used to dominate the Walled Garden. Its spreading domed branch structure dangled hundreds of winged seed cases, like threaded green necklaces, beneath the Ash-like foliage. The knarred and burred trunk was 8 m in circumference and described as looking like 'Treebeard', an Ent from *The Lord of the Rings*.

It had been planted around 1850, most likely from a batch of

Felling the giant Wingnut tree in 2011.

seedlings introduced by William Fox-Strangways, the 4th Earl of Ilchester, who had connections in the Caucasus where these magnificent trees are indigenous. It had perhaps grown so well because its roots had tapped into the underground culvert, which was providing a constant supply of flowing spring water. Unfortunately the tree was slowly dying from fungal attack to its central core and root system and it had to be felled in 2011. Another huge specimen still remains in the Gardens.

Many of the large Holm Oak trees growing in the Gardens are from the original early 19th-century plantings and thus are at least 170 years old. They originate from the Mediterranean. They are good shade bearers and there is no

Felling the giant Wingnut tree in 2011.

better tree for the architectural backbone of a garden or park. The name 'Holm' (and also the Latin name *Quercus ilex*) means holly, in reference to the evergreen leaves which when young are spiny. The timber itself is very dense and quite heavy and makes a good slow-burning firewood. In the past some of the trees had been pollarded, which most likely extended their life.

In 2000 we pollarded the Holm Oaks that run the length of the roadside near the main entrance. The timber stumps looked quite ugly for a time until the new growth began to appear. This success has been repeated around the Gardens, even to the extent that we have kept the regrowth clipped to form new shelter hedges around the site.

Woodland gardens are a haven for pests and pathogens, all waiting to take hold. Honey Fungus (*Armillaria*) is often present, ready to spread to any weak, old or decaying tree or shrub, and even quite healthy plants can be affected. Another fungal disease that really took hold in Abbotsbury in the 1970s was notorious Dutch Elm disease. The Gardens and indeed the village lost all their ancient Elm tree specimens. There are positive moves to plant the more disease-tolerant species Wytch Elm (*Ulmus gladbra*). However, as one devastating pathogen is 'managed', another takes its place. Today Abbotsbury and many other gardens, particularly in the South West, are facing a new threat from the fungal spores of *Phytophtora ramorum*, sometimes known as Sudden Oak Death. A water- and air-borne fungal disease that threatens many trees and shrubs, to date there is no known cure and it is being controlled by digging up and burning infected plants. A more widely publicised on-going problem is Ash Dieback (caused by *Chalara fraxinia*) which results in leaf loss, crown dieback and bark lesions in affected trees. It is usually fatal, either directly or indirectly by weakening the tree to the point where it succumbs more readily to attack by other pests or pathogens, especially Honey Fungus. Luckily Abbotsbury has only a few large Ash specimens, which have so far escaped any dieback.

Using Tirfor winches to move trees and pull roots, 1999.

Where trees need felling because they are diseased or dangerous ideally the stumps need to be removed as well, as they may harbour fungal problems or simply take up space for new planting. When the stump is not too large it is possible to dig around and axe the main roots, then attach a steel cable from a Tirfor winch to pull it out. Access to the Gardens is restricted by the narrow footpaths, but whenever possible a stump grinder machine would always be the first choice.

Grey squirrels can strip the bark off saplings and girdle (ring bark) trees. Young buck Roe Deer will also strip bark off young trees whilst scent-marking their territory. Rabbits and moles have caused much damage over the years in young plantations and borders. Poor planting of trees in the first place can account for the early death of some plants. Tree stems planted too deeply can cause premature rotting in the trunk, or trees not firmed in enough around the root can cause the roots to dry out and even increase damage from 'wind rock' of the whole plant.

Many of our mature trees become 'wind pruned'. The top branches of their crowns are more stunted and hold lots of dead wood. Winter gales in particular carry salt-laden air from the sea over the tree canopy. The tallest conifers such as the Californian Redwood *Sequoia sempervirens* have their tops scorched brown and it can take all summer to recover before the cycle begins next winter.

With the ever-increasing threat of litigation in public places, we carry out scheduled Tree Surveys, where every tree is numbered and tagged with a risk assessment and identification of potential further tree care.

In 2008 one of our tallest Oak trees, at over 120 ft, fell down, crashing through and destroying smaller trees and shrubs on its way. Living for many years surrounded by a thicket of running Bamboo (*Sasa palmatum*), the Oak was found to be riddled with the black boot-laces of Honey Fungus, yet its canopy and leaves all looked in good condition. We counted the annual growth rings at its base, which put the planting date at *c* 1840. This was around the time that the 3rd Earl of Ilchester was actively planting new woodland. The fallen Oak could have been removed but it was decided to make it a feature. A chainsaw carver and artist was brought in to discuss ideas. Two scenes were designed for either side of the main trunk and carved seats were created from a fork, making an ideal resting point for groups undertaking guided tours.

Chainsaw artist Matthew Crab carving animals in a fallen Oak tree.

A natural way to welcome visitors, and politely educate.

In places like Borneo, many of the National Park rainforest entrances have timber signs welcoming the visitor with a subtle message about the environment. We decided to do something similar, using the Oak offcuts.

We had the wettest summer for many years in 2012, and a huge specimen Monterey Cypress tree with a top-heavy crown, standing at over 120 ft, became waterlogged at the roots. The tree fell without warning during the night and slid down the slope into the Top Pond. The crown filled the pond and covered the surrounding paths. It took several weeks to clear during the winter, but as it was so substantial we left the trunk and hollowed out pockets for planting ferns and bromeliads to create a 'jungle look'.

Uprooted Monterey Cypress, July 2012.

Fallen Monterey Cypress, 2012.

Ponds and Streams

Photos taken in 1889 show the Lily ponds, which sit high on the ironstone ridge north west of the Gardens, heavily planted with *Phormiums, Yuccas, Cordylines* and Pampas grasses, all quite new to British cultivation at the time. The ornate lead water duct that feeds water into the ponds is dated 1815, so it probably came from the well in the Sunken Lawn which predates the ponds.

The Lily ponds in 1898. (Courtesy of Country Life Illustrated.)

Lead well head feeding the Lily ponds.

In 1991 the ponds were looking tired. Over the years the Holm Oaks that surround them had become overcrowded, with branches that hung over the water, making it dark and shady. Being 'evergreen', they shed their coarse leaves each June, which over many years filled up the ponds. The slow microbiotic breakdown in the water gives off a rich dark tannin which de-oxygenates the water and kills the fish. There was no planting left around the ponds as the soil had eroded away, leaving a shallow iron-rich subsoil. There was a constant trickle of water running from the sides of the stone work, leaving the largest pond always half empty.

First, selective tree surgery and crown reduction work was carried out to let in more light. Then the largest Lily pond was emptied of water and fish, followed by days of hard shovelling to remove the metre-deep silt,

Restored Lily ponds.

sludge, leaves and twigs. A long-lasting butyl liner was added, its top edges capped with old house bricks to hide it. Raised stone planting beds were created around the sides of the pond and soil was brought in from around the Gardens to fill them up. The planting was designed to echo some of the plants that were identified in the early 1898 photographs.

For over a hundred years the overflow water from the ponds was piped underground and gravity-fed down the hillside to pour out unused into the main stream that runs the length of the valley. Many Italian historic gardens

Taro (Colocasia esculenta), with its exotic leaves, manages to grow successfully outside in a shallow stream without winter protection.

from the 17th century, and indeed Chatsworth House, have 'water staircases'. A series of stone steps are built into a hillside and water is pumped out over the top step, cascading in sheets of silvery water that catch the light. This simple effective design was applied to the Abbotsbury Lily ponds on a modest scale. Outflow water was diverted into a catchment pool, to then flow overland down an old disused flight of steps. This cascade area has been planted with moisture-loving plants, South African Restio reeds and even Taro from Asia, *Colocasia esculenta*. The stream has become a refuge for wildlife, with many birds coming to drink, frogs spawning in the shallows, and Damselflies darting in and out of the reeds.

In the Woodland Valley three larger ponds were also restored by digging out tons of silt. This time a small digger and dumper truck were used.

The cast-iron sluice gates that used to control the water flow in

Wall lizards can often be found in the Gardens.

Pond clearance by hand.

the main ponds had to be rebuilt by a local blacksmith. The biggest challenge though was to improve the streamside and bring it back to its former glory. The cool shelter, humidity and moist, rich organic soil of the streamside provide the perfect setting for drifts of colourful Primulas, large-leaved foliage plants and flowing grasses. However, left unchecked two dominant species had taken over – the notorious Japanese Knotweed and Butterbur.

Planting stream-sides in 1998.

Mature water-sides looking glorious today.

Continuous hand digging and spraying for almost 3 years was the only way to ensure this area was clear of these invasive plants.

Musa basjoo, *the banana plant.*

Primulas have now become naturalised, *Rodgersia* and *Astilbes* have established, and giant *Gunnera* leaves and tropical-looking Japanese Bananas combine to add seasonal interest.

Near the Bothy the stream runs under the wall of the Walled Garden into a series of small pools. These were Victorian silt traps, designed to catch the sediment in the water and prevent it silting up the larger Woodland

Valley ponds. In 1990 they were completely full so were dug out and the wooden sluice gates replaced.

With really heavy rain from winter storms, the stream cannot cope with the torrents of water that thunder down the hillside, which sometimes flooded the road and entered the shop. As an extra precaution we created a new large silt trap in the stream across the access road, outside the Gardens. It has an overflow ditch to divert excess flood water away into the fields.

Summer flooding, July 2012.

Restored sluice gate and working silt trap

Facilities for Visitors

By 1992 visitor numbers were rising. From the outset, plans had been drawn up from a series of meetings with John Houston (General Manager, Abbotsbury Tourism), the land agent Edward Green and the accountants regarding any future capital investment in the Gardens. One of the biggest concerns was finding ways to attract more coach tours to the area, as they were a vital source of income.

It became apparent that although people were keen to visit and enjoy the Gardens, many were travelling for several hours and on arrival their main concern was the all-important comfort stop, or more crudely a 'P and a T'! The Tea Garden as it stood was very outdated. It resembled a shanty town of little wooden huts, one serving hot drinks and sandwiches, another a garden shed shelter. The biggest eyesore was the antiquated toilet block with no hot water or electricity. There were also two small wooden aviaries nearby, housing budgies and cockatiels, that were constructed in the 1960s – and they looked it. The Gardens would benefit from a restaurant with professional catering serving hot food.

The old Tea Garden, with Caucasian Wingnut tree in the background.

In 1997 I received a Winston Churchill Memorial Trust travel scholarship. This was a grant to carry out research in any subject to benefit a person's career and the local community. I applied for 'Garden History and Development'. The plan was to visit Mediterranean gardens and nurseries in France and Italy and carry out voluntary work in Jerusalem Botanical Gardens. I came away with fresh ideas about garden development that included buildings, infrastructure and design. In particular I felt an Old Colonial style would suit Abbotsbury well. The Gardens have a history closely connected with plant hunting and new plant introductions from around the world. The exotic nature of architectural plants like Palm trees and Bamboos add that continental flavour, so it seemed appropriate that we have a restaurant building in that character.

Initial sketches with a wooden veranda and tin roof were developed by local architect David Shaw and after some deliberation approval was gained, even for the red tin roof which we felt might be a sticking point. The only issue was English Heritage insisting that the 18th-century Grade I listed Walled Garden wall could

Construction begins on the new restaurant, 1997.

not be disturbed, meaning all building materials would have to be craned over it. Before construction took place the demolition of the existing old toilet block, sheds and aviary had priority along with the removal of any rescuable plants.

A few years later it was felt we had got the style exactly right. The Colonial Restaurant beautifully complements the subtropical theme and atmosphere of the Gardens.

The Colonial Restaurant today.

The West Lawn

The 1990 storm left a scene of devastation on the hillside at the back of the West Lawn. Where once stood a dark Holm Oak wood, with nesting wood pigeons, there was now a vast area of fallen trees. It was like witnessing the aftermath of some forest battlefield, with huge trunks uprooted and lying prostrate amongst the grass. Several weeks of chain-sawing and timber hauling followed, and tractors were used to push some of the root balls back into the ground. Years later they have grown new shoots and a new crown. Holm Oaks are remarkable trees. Some can live for years without rotting.

Perhaps the greatest benefit of the storm damage was that the Gardens became much lighter and less gloomy, enabling many more plant species to be planted where the sun shines through. The West Lawn is now a practical open area ideal for holding events, with marquees and even a stage for performers.

The West Lawn has increased in size since a bold decision was taken to demolish the old Conservatory. This was a Victorian-style glass house that had only been built in 1986. Robin Herbert, President of the RHS at the time and a cousin of the present owner of the Gardens, Mrs Townshend, officially opened it. However, it was suffering from severe rot in the timbers and costing a lot of money, time and effort to upkeep. Also it did not look in keeping and dominated the area. Moreover, its internal dimensions were restrictive and beds very small, which prevented really good-impact planting.

It was removed in 1998. The main cast-iron upright supporting legs were saved and later used in the new entrance pergola, where they now have pride of place supporting the wooden beams and climbing plants right by

the roadside and shop. The Lawn often used to sit waterlogged in winter, so after dismantling the Conservatory a network of drainage pipes was installed to take excess water away to a main drain.

The West Lawn in 1991, with the old Conservatory.

Birds in the Garden

Peacocks were introduced to the Gardens in the 1960s and quickly become a major visitor attraction. However, their numbers increased significantly to about twenty by 1990 and they were eating the soft new growth of tender plants, trampling emerging ground cover and deposited unwelcome droppings on the seats in the Tea Garden. There is a place for birds in a woodland garden and they do add another element of surprise whilst walking through, so the peacocks were rehomed and Golden Pheasants introduced instead.

The colourful Pheasants in the Gardens allow visitors to get quite close to them.

Lemon Golden Pheasant.

In the Walled Garden was a rather sad-looking aviary with budgies and cockatiels in quite a small space. We rehoused the birds and removed the aviary, and in its place installed a traditional wall-mounted dovecote, with two pairs of Tumbling Doves. It was envisaged they would add some drama as these wonderful birds dropped from the sky. After a couple of weeks they were settled in and displaying wonderfully, but one by one they disappeared. The culprit was a Sparrowhawk.

All of the senses can benefit from a garden visit, and with the

Kookaburra and chicks.

peacocks we had lost their haunting cry. During a visit to Harewood House Gardens in North Yorkshire in 1995 I heard the incredibly distinctive and jungle-like call of their Laughing Kookaburras. We introduced a breeding pair from the Rhode Bird Gardens near Bath and they have been a wonderful addition to our Subtropical Gardens.

Kookaburras, introduced in 1995.

Golden Pheasants.

The Bothy

On the north-east-facing wall of the Walled Garden, built into the wall itself, is a tiny one-up one-down building known as the Bothy. In the early 19th century this type of building provided basic comfortless accommodation. The Bothy was said to have originated from Scottish farms providing accommodation for unmarried ploughmen. The idea was taken up by large country estate gardens when housing began to be needed for the large number of single gardeners, improvers and journeymen whose homes were beyond walking distance, and for apprentice gardeners who would learn the trade by living on site.

Part of their routine would be to get up early in winter to stoke the boilers of the stove houses, wash clay pots and clean wooden seed boxes. Many bothies had no bathroom and made use of the stove tank to get water that came from the roof. With black beetles on the floor and three to a bed, the duty boy at the end was likely to be kicked out in the early hours to go to the boiler house and stoke the fires to keep the stove house warm. An article written in the 1 February 1902 issue of *The Garden* magazine had the courage to highlight the conditions of life in the Bothy:

> *The horses in the stable are more comfortably housed than the young gardeners in the Bothy. Young gardeners do not look for the comforts of a home, but neither do they expect to live in a cow shed.*

By 1990 the Bothy at Abbotsbury was a rotting shell, the roof leaked, and rising damp and floodwater had made it totally uninhabitable. We had to preserve this historic little building. Whilst restoring it in 1995 we uncovered an upstairs fireplace behind the brickwork, as well as the main fireplace in the living room. At one time the upper floor had been a cool, dark fruit store for apples and pears, on wooden shelves. The timbers in the roof indicated that the building was originally thatched, most likely using reed from our own Swannery down the road. The upstairs room was full of cobwebs, rotting rafters, woodworm-infested seed boxes, old tools and rusty old tins with lethal chemicals oozing through. One contained Cymag, a deadly, fast-acting poison which releases cyanide on contact with moisture

The old Bothy, now a museum.

and was once used to control rabbits and moles, and some care was needed to dispose of it safely.

Although the building was a simple affair we thought it could be used as an opportunity to exhibit all the old gardening tools as a sort of museum. We had unearthed many old rakes, hoes, spades, potato shovels and ancient secateurs. Once news got out that we were collecting old garden tools several items were donated to the collection, including a wooden yoke and a beautifully preserved seed fiddle. The blacksmith from Langton Herring turned up with an unusual pair of edging shears with a built-in roller designed to take the weight of the shears, and a neighbour gave us his father's leather gaiters to put on show.

Interpretation and Botanical Data

Signage in a large garden open to the public is a vital tool for communication and education and a visual aid for direction. We currently use a series of white arrows to help direct visitors along the best route. Plants with seasonal interest have dedicated information notice boards that are positioned when the plant is at its best, flowering or in full fruit, describing the specific points of interest. There are mixed thoughts on having labels with Latin and common names attached to plants. Botanical gardens are there to educate and inform the public with stories and information about the plants' economic, social, medicinal or environmental uses. Therefore labels are considered a necessity.

Privately owned gardens open to the public sometimes take the view that any form of labelling can detract from the plants' beauty and add clutter to a garden's character. At Abbotsbury we aim to keep a regular update of plant labels as requested by the public, yet keeping labels to the minimum to avoid repetition throughout the Gardens. In the past, labels were nailed to trees without enough spacing allowed for growth, and pretty soon the woody cambium layer, immediately below the bark, can engulf old nails and even labels if they have been neglected. Using specially made bed stands to hold the label is preferred, or if the tree trunk is the only option then a nail with a small spring behind it and plenty of slack will give the label and tree some growing space.

Neglected labelling.

Keeping plant records for Abbotsbury has been a hit and miss affair in the past. Apart from the privately printed list of plants at Abbotsbury in 1898 there is little historical and botanical information about the Gardens in the archives. In the 1970s a card index system was used to record all new plants in the garden, but it did not take in the existing ancient specimens and many plants on file have long since died and not been removed from the index, making the system pretty much outdated.

June Beckinsale using the old brass plate Pantograph machine to engrave plant labels.

Today we use a computer database specifically written for botanical gardens. There are fields for accession numbers, country of origin, plant source, plant family and much more. This information is then used for future plant labels. It means a lot of time spent taking records in the Gardens, for both old and new plants, and collating the data will take many years but will provide an excellent archive for the future.

Through networking with other professional establishments such as the Royal Botanic Gardens at Kew, Wakehurst Place, RBG Edinburgh and RHS Wisley it has been possible to obtain plants from more recent collections in countries like Korea, China and Taiwan. Many of these plants will not be available to the nursery trade and will be rare in cultivation. Each comes with its own individually listed accession number, GPS location, and details of the altitude and regional and geographical terrain, and even the weather conditions when the botanist collected the seed. However, restrictions on plant movement may change in the future as tighter legislation on the distribution of introduced plants takes effect.

Vistas and Focal Points

Visitors to a garden should enjoy the ambience, take in the floral displays, colourful shrubs, trees and borders, and indulge in self-awareness of the environment around them. A good garden should have a relaxed atmosphere. Space is not just a physical dimension; it is more a matter of how you feel. Surprise views, distant vistas and focal points in the landscape all contribute to the overall 'feel good factor'.

Moving statues.

An article written about Abbotsbury Gardens in an 1898 issue of *Country Life* magazine described the many fine views from the Gardens, taking in 13th-century St Catherine's Chapel that sits on a hillside looking out to sea. By 1997 one could only just glimpse the Chapel through the sparse winter foliage. Tree surgeons were brought in to carefully

'Window-frame' view of St Catherine's Chapel.

cut out a 'window frame' through the canopy, creating a magnificent vista from a strategically placed bench.

This was of course not a new idea. In 1750 Capability Brown had already been incorporating his vision of vistas in the garden, with designs that 'Bring the countryside to the garden' and create views to distant landscapes or church spires.

Rustic bridge. (From Country Life Illustrated *1898.)*

The woodland garden surrounds the little stream that flows down the valley. Pictures taken in 1899 show rustic bridges crossing the stream that were made from weathered tree branches woven into attractive hand rails.

In 1995 three new Oriental-style foot bridges were installed. We painted them brick red to counter the predominantly green background and create a focal point for photographers.

The winding pathways and undulating slopes in the Gardens can mislead visitors. Some even ask for directions back to the entrance. A lack of shelter was also identified,

One of the Oriental-style bridges installed in 1995 and restored in 2013.

particularly with larger groups. The Sino-Himalayan Glade is one of the furthest points from the entrance and it used to have a wooden shelter for about three people. In 1995 we replaced this with a rather grand summerhouse designed in a pseudo-Victorian/ Chinese style. This provides a tranquil resting place with seating for large groups and also creates another focal point.

Summerhouse built in 1995.

In the north-west corner of the Gardens there is a sheltered section of the original 18th-century wall. This site once had a collection of old shrub roses, clipped parterre box hedging and an ugly metal water tank. Overshadowing by Holm Oak and Elm trees had caused all the plants to become leggy and poor flowering. This south-facing wall was being wasted, as it was hidden in deep shade, and we really needed to have a focal point such as a garden sculpture or ornate building to draw the eye from two distant viewpoints.

First it was decided to fell some of the trees blocking the sunlight, then we took out untidy shrubs obscuring the storm ditch that runs below the corner of the walls. The renowned landscape garden designer and Vice Chairman of the RHS Martin Lane Fox was commissioned to draw up plans for a garden building or folly to enhance the area. His brief was to make a solid-oak structure that could function as a seating area and open shelter. This Oak Pavilion (unofficially known as 'Fox's Folly') was constructed by the Ilchester Estates' own building department in 2005 using Oak grown on the Estate. Precise dimensions in height and scale were needed to achieve the right proportions as a distant vista.

The Oak Pavilion has by chance become a favourite with couples as a site to say their marriage vows. The Gardens has a civil marriage licence for outdoor weddings, which have gained in popularity, as the setting can be quite stunning.

The Gardens benefit from the maritime climate because of their close proximity to the sea. For over two centuries Abbotsbury Gardens has nestled in a sheltered valley, with a steep hillside dividing the woodland from the sea. When the wind blows from the south west, the storm beach

Oak Pavilion, finished in 2005. The building's classical outline works as a focal point to draw the eye from distant points in the Gardens.

The Gardens are licensed for civil marriages and the Oak Pavilion is the first choice for couples to get married in. In this photo Abbotsbury gardener Tim Newman marries Hannah at a ceremony in January 2013. The impromptu garden staff 'Guard of honour' is provided by (left to right) Sean Boast, Mark Sheldon, Charles Leeming and Stephen Griffith.

picks up the sea and stone shingle in mighty swells that thump and crash as the waves hit the beach. The waves can be heard in the Gardens and when winter gales blow one can even smell the salt in the air. On many occasions I have walked up through the surrounding woodland, out from the Gardens boundary to the top of the hill. Here is one of the best views of the entire Chesil Beach, including the Swannery on the Fleet, Portland Bill to the east and Golden

Cap to the west. I thought it would make a fantastic viewpoint if we could extend the Gardens up here.

In 2001 the Dorset and East Devon coastline was officially designated a World Heritage Site, named the Jurassic Coast because of its geology and the fossils found in the area. This was now an important factor in the tourism of the area and an added bonus, given that the Gardens are pretty much right in the middle of it. After much consultation with Mrs Townshend and trustees it was decided to create an opening through the woodland for a footpath of modest dimensions. As we tackled the undergrowth, fallen trees and scrub, the clearing to the hilltop began to emerge.

Clearing the hillside ready for planting magnolias, January 2007.

To enclose this new Jurassic View Point, stone was used from an old quarry in the village to match the existing dry-stone wall.

It soon became apparent that the scale of the operation needed to be ramped up if it were to make an impact on the landscape. Sir Simon Hornby endorsed this, and we decided to plant an avenue of *Magnolia campbellii*, Sir Simon's favourite shrub. An earlier visit to Mount Congreve Gardens in Waterford, Ireland, had provided inspiration as there is an attractive Magnolia avenue running through that garden. We planted them flanking the grassy slope of the hillside, envisaging the wonderful pink blossom each spring. Later, Jim Gardiner (Curator of RHS Wisley and the author of a book entitled *Magnolias*) gave further advice on cultivars. The form called 'Wisley' was grown and grafted for us by Peter Catt, who is a renowned nurseryman and expert propagator. We also planted *M. campbellii* 'Leonard Messel'. An outer planting of *M.* × *soulangeana* 'Brozzonii' was used which will come into flower earlier, whilst the *M. campbellii* will need many years to reach flowering. The only concern was to keep the rabbits and deer away from the young trees whilst they matured.

New grass seed was sown and drainage incorporated to help make the area less slippery. Each autumn for several years the gardeners planted thousands of Daffodils to increase the colourful springtime experience and form a carpet beneath the young Magnolias. The old cannons originally from Abbotsbury Castle grounds were brought up from the West Lawn, as it seemed more fitting to have them face out to sea again.

A steep haul uphill between the surrounding woodland but worth it. Looking east from the View Point.

The Jurassic Garden.

At the bottom of the Woodland Valley in a damp area by the pond we created a 'Jurassic Garden' to link with the theme of the Jurassic Coast. By growing plant species that have been found in fossils and planting large evergreen foliage, it has taken on a swampy primeval appearance.

Garden Events and Publicity

By the 1950s much of the Gardens had become an overgrown wilderness, yet it provided a wonderful playground for the village children. Ilchester Estates had been subsidising running costs for many years, but after the storm of January 1990 the time had come to turn it around into a business that at least met all its own running costs. Apart from ongoing maintenance and improvements, we looked for other ways to increase visitor numbers and new audiences.

In July 1990 the first event organised was a barn dance in the Tea Garden, where refreshments, seating and a barbeque were available. The band 'English Mustard' employed a caller to get the dances under way and untangle the dancers.

A retail plant centre and nursery was also set up in 1990. It was established as a unique 'plantsman's nursery' full of choice and rare plants, but we were always looking for ways to promote it. We took up an invitation to exhibit at the local Aldon Horse Trials equestrian event near Yeovil. As well as a stall selling plants we sponsored one of the large horse jumps. The commentator announced the horse and rider as approaching the 'Abbotsbury Gardens Jump' loud and clear for all to hear – inspirational marketing. This event was a real eye-opener for creating more plant sales.

In 1993 the Royal Horticultural Society took over the running of Hampton Court Palace Flower Show, in which we entered a subtropical plant display. We were awarded a Silver-Gilt Medal for the design and quality of plants, but also sold over £3,500 worth of plants. The following year we exhibited at the Chelsea

Planting by Abbotsbury Gardens at Chelsea Flower Show.

Flower Show with Marshall James. Transporting landscape materials and people to and from London was more difficult logistically, but again well worth it as we were awarded a silver award and plenty of publicity.

The Swannery was holding its 600th Centenary Festival in 1993. The open field in front of the Swannery was transformed into a medieval jousting arena. We provided our version of a medieval plant stand, selling herbs for remedies and ailments. Our rather novel 'Maggot Racing' stall run by the Gardens staff was also hugely popular.

In 1992, having seen how some National Trust properties use their gardens for summer theatre productions, we booked a touring group from the Bristol Royal Vic Youth National Theatre. They performed Shakespeare's *A Midsummer's Night Dream* and the balmy July evening on the West Lawn was perfect for the 150 visitors. We helped the production team set up a basic stage with props and provided straw bales from the farm for seating. The Royal Vic backstage team provided professional theatrical lighting that shone through the trees to create a magical setting. This sparked an idea that would later be developed into one of our biggest annual events – our 'Soleil Lumiere' or 'Enchanted Floodlit Gardens' event. Coloured floodlights provide up-lighting through the trees to highlight the autumn leaf colours and architectural shapes of exotic Palm trees and Bamboos.

Autumn illuminations by Stephen Banks.

This event runs annually from October through to November, timed for attracting visitors during the half-term school holiday. We were now developing a strategy for events in the Gardens through trial and error. For several years we held a Garden Festival with a floral marquee, plant stands and handicrafts. The trouble was that every other town in the area had similar events going on and visitor numbers suffered. As it became less cost effective to set up and run we decided to abandon the event. In 2006 John Houston located a travelling 'French market' which set up on the West Lawn with stalls full of traditional farm produce. Another year we rented a marquee for a somewhat unusual 'Clairvoyants and spiritual readings' event.

Pink Magnolia blossom in spring.

The Woodland Valley in springtime is a riot of colour. Bold shades of pink petals crown the bare stems of Magnolias and the Camellias compete with branches laden with flowers.

At this time of year, around the Spring Bank Holiday, we hold a 'Giant Easter Egg Hunt', which has become popular with families with young children, some of whom might not otherwise have ventured out on a visit. Other light entertainment has been added to this over the years, such as the musical sounds of a hurdy gurdy, magicians, jugglers, face painting and Morris men. Like many other botanical gardens, Abbotsbury offers additional interpretation with woodland trails and children's quizzes to keep younger visitors occupied, involved and hopefully interested.

Morris men at the annual Easter Egg Hunt.

Every July the Gardens play host for one day to the musical duo of Steve Knightly and Phil Beer, known as 'Show of Hands'. They are one of the UK's best traditional acoustic music and singer-song writing partnerships. The

'Show of Hands' summer concert 2010.

West Lawn becomes the main arena, where we can get full capacity of up to 1,500 visitors, and all tickets are generally sold in advance. The Gardens have also been used by film crews.

Filming a BBC costume drama of an Edwardian tea party set in Burma with actor Geoffrey Palmer.

Royal Visits and Connections

HRH Princess Charlotte of Wales, granddaughter of King George III and Queen Charlotte, stayed at Gloucester Lodge on the promenade in Weymouth in October 1814. It was a popular belief that to bathe in seawater would cure many ailments and that it would heal her painful knee. During her stay she visited Abbotsbury Castle and Gardens accompanied by Countess Rosslyn and Countess Ilchester. On 12 October 1814 *The Morning Post* reported her visit to Melbury House, the seat of Lord and Lady Ilchester:

> *Arriving by barouche … the Royal party were received with the most distinguished marks of respect and after partaking of an elegant cold collation, returned that evening to Gloucester Lodge.*

(A *barouche* was a horse-drawn summer carriage fashionable in the 19th century.)

In October 1817 the 3rd Earl of Ilchester played host at Melbury to the recently married Duke and Duchess of Gloucester.

On 19 August 1846 Queen Victoria and Prince Albert arrived at Weymouth on the Royal Yacht. The following is an extract from the *Dorset County Chronicle*:

> *After being welcomed ashore at Weymouth, Her Majesty and the Royal party proceeded in carriages and four to Abbotsbury Castle, one of the seats of the Right Hon the Earl of Ilchester. Her Majesty made but a brief inspection of the Castle and grounds at Abbotsbury, with which she was pleased to express her gratification; the Swannery was also an object of particular interest to the Queen. The Royal party returned to Weymouth about 7pm.*

The *Daily News* on 22 August 1846 reported:

> *Her Majesty's visit was unexpected and no preparations were made in her honour as the Earl of Ilchester was unfortunately at sea in his yacht, the* Petrel. *The Royal party, however, visited the Gardens and were conducted by Mr Nicholson, his Lordship's gardener. Her Majesty was pleased with the taste displayed in the arrangements of the gardens. The visitors returned to Weymouth after visiting*

the swannery, and re-embarked on board their yacht. The squadron set sail for Plymouth the next day.

In 1992 a box of glass-plate photographs was given to the Estate, dating from around 1900. This provides an insight into village life at the turn of the century, with clear images of buildings, landscapes and people.

Abbotsbury village c 1900.

Gardening Class at Abbotsbury School c 1920. Most of the children are wearing their father's caps.

Carriage outside the Ilchester Arms in Abbotsbury village 8 Dec 1904 with HRH Princess of Wales and Lady Stavordale.

There were also many postcards printed from these plates. Several depict a Royal visit by HRH Prince and Princess of Wales in 1904. In those days visitors arrived by steam train from Weymouth, alighting at the small station in Abbotsbury, and were then taken by horse and carriage around the village. There was even a train named after the village.

From left: Lady Ilchester, Sir Donald Wallace, Lady Powis, Lady Guinness, HRH Princess of Wales and Lady Crewe, 8 December 1904.

The 'Luncheon Ground' is a raised levelled lawn at the top of the valley, rather like a golf tee area. This site would have commanded fine views over the Gardens and out to St Catherine's Chapel. A marquee was always erected for special occasions, as a base for the shooting party to take lunch. Later, Lady Mary and Henry Edward Fox-Strangways, the 5th Earl of Ilchester, planted a large avenue of Monterey Pines (*Pinus radiata*) in commemoration of King George V's Coronation on 22 June 1911. The date was confirmed by counting the trunk rings of dead trees felled from this avenue in 2005.

Marquee on Abbotsbury 'Luncheon Ground', with HRH Prince of Wales (later King, George V), 8 Dec 1904. The Royal couple came to join a shooting party organised by the Earl of Ilchester, and members of aristocratic families, dignitaries and local worthies took part.

Abbotsbury Swannery at the head of the Fleet lagoon lies behind Chesil Beach. It is a Site of Special Scientific Interest (SSSI) and has been under ownership of the Strangways family for fifteen generations. It was once owned by Abbotsbury Benedictine monastery and the monks who lived there managed the swans as a ready source of meat up until 1539. Today it is a major tourist attraction and the swans have become accustomed to the presence of visitors.

In 1993 during the 600th centenary festivities, the Royal Mail produced a special gold First-Day Cover centenary stamp featuring Abbotsbury swans.

HRH Prince Charles's visit in 1993, with Head Gardener Stephen Griffith and the Honourable Charlotte Townshend.

ABBOTSBURY.
THE ROYAL VISIT TO ABBOTSBURY.

The Prince of Wales accompanied by Lord Ilchester and shooting party arrived at Abbotsbury at 9.40 by special train from Melbury and were conveyed by carriages with postillions, motors, &c., to the Langton end of the Fleet Water where they went on board the new boats specially made for the occasion and the coote drive at once commenced. There being many thousands of them there was a continuance of brisk shooting until the Swannery was reached. Then the wild fowl shooting commenced as also did snipe and woodcock, of which they killed a large number. The royal party then went to the celebrated gardens where luncheon was served in a large marquee specially provided for the occasion. The marquee, carpeting and seating were provided by the well-known Dorchester manufacturer, Mr. R. B. Brown.

The Princess accompanied by the House party had arrived by the 11.40 special. On leaving the station H.R.H. entered a carriage driven by a pair of horses, with postillions, accompanied by Lady Stavordale, the Duchess of Marlborough, &c. By special request, Mr. T. Cooper, proprietor of the Ilchester Hotel, accompanied them on the box seat of the carriage to point out the different places of interest en route. On leaving the station the Royal party went first direct to the Hotel where Her Royal Highness made a brief stay without alighting to insert her name in the visitors book (which contains many Royal signatures), and Her Royal Highness graciously accepted from Mr. Cooper a copy of the "Guide to Abbotsbury," of which he is author. The presentation was made by Mrs. T. Cooper. The party then drove to the famous Swannery, the monastery ruins, and other places, Mr. Cooper proving an able cicerone On arriving at the swing gate H.R.H. specially thanked Mr. Cooper for his attention. At the Swannery, H.R.H. met the shooting party, and explored the celebrated Swannery, decoy, &c. The shooting after luncheon was at the Castle coverts, under the direction of Mr. Wren, his lordship's headkeeper. The Prince fully justified his reputation as an expert shot, the birds flying exceedingly high. Shooting over, the Royal Party partook of tea at the Castle, and left by the 5.10 special train for Melbury. The village of Abbotsbury was gaily decorated, and as the royal visitors passed the school they were enthusiastically greeted by the children and a large crowd.

Newspaper cutting from Southern Times, *10 December 1904.*

We were also delighted to host a surprise visit by HRH Prince Charles to the Swannery and Gardens for this special occasion. It was a real honour to meet and greet HRH and lead him around the Gardens on a tour, along with Mrs Townshend and the High Sheriff of Dorset Richard Guy Grosvenor De Pelet and other distinguished guests. The Gardens were open to the public as usual and it was interesting to see the look on visitors' faces. HRH's helicopter landed on the village cricket pitch, causing quite a stir, before he was chauffeured to the Gardens in a black Bentley decorated with union jack flags on each wing mirror and the bonnet.

Garland Day

Since the early 19th century, Garland Day celebrations have taken place in Abbotsbury village on 13 May (Old May Day). They were mentioned by John Hutchins in his book *The History and Antiquities of the County of Dorset* (1861–73). Traditionally the custom involved the making of flower garlands by local children whose families were fishermen. The garlands were blessed in a church service and some were then rowed out to sea and tossed into the water as a donation to the sea gods. This marked the opening of the fishing season, and the children then played games and danced on the beach.

Sometime after World War I, children from non-fishing families began to take part, probably due to the decline in the fishing industry. The school gave the children a day's holiday whilst they paraded around the village with garlands raised on two poles. One garland was made from wild flowers and the other from garden flowers, usually collected from the Gardens. The aim was for the children to collect money to keep.

Abbotsbury village Garland Day, May 1935. (Photo © S.J. Herbert.)

In 1954 the local policeman decided that children collecting pennies constituted begging and he impounded the children and garlands. Furious mothers complained and the Fox-Strangways family took up the matter.

Clare James keeping the Garland Day tradition going in 2011.

The children were released and the policeman was reprimanded, with apologies from the Chief Constable. Local villages have since shown a strong determination to maintain this old English tradition.

Ilchester Estates

Working for a large country business like Ilchester Estates can be very rewarding. A real mix of diverse businesses contribute to the stewardship of the countryside and help the rural economy and these have played an important role for hundreds of years, providing a steady revenue that is reinvested in managing the historic landscape.

Farming, game-keeping and forestry are the more traditional departments within the Estate. Tourism now plays an important role also. Abbotsbury Tourism consists of the Subtropical Gardens, Swannery (home to over 600 mute swans) and Children's Farm at the historic 14th-century thatched Tithe Barn.

Abbotsbury Swannery nesting time, with Swanherd Gregory Gill, c 1914.

Ilchester Estates' property portfolio adds to these key businesses. The Estate's local property interests were once much bigger. In 1914 the 6th Earl of Ilchester sold off a 15-acre plot of building land at West Bay, where the West Cliff Estate stands today, and the Estate also once included the entire village of Shipton Gorge. At 8 miles long, the Fleet, which runs from Abbotsbury to Ferry Bridge where it opens into Portland Harbour, is the largest tidal lagoon in the UK. The bed of the Fleet has been owned by the Estate since 1539 and to this day the Estate still manages the Fleet nature reserve. All rights to wrecking have long since been waived!

Melbury House is the private family home set in beautiful open parkland. It has been a managed deer park since 1549. The Estate office and accounts department is based there and it is the headquarters of all the Estate's businesses. The annual staff Christmas party is held in the Library at the House and is one of the few times when all departments get to mingle. Another tradition used to be the annual cricket match.

Melbury and Abbotsbury cricket teams, 1992.

The following is a list of Abbotsbury Head Gardeners and Estate Owners since 1765.

Year	Head Gardener	Estate Owner
1765	Not recorded	1st Countess of Ilchester – Elizabeth Fox-Strangways
1776	Not recorded	2nd Earl of Ilchester – Henry Thomas Fox-Strangways
1808	Mr Nicholson	3rd Earl of Ilchester – Henry Stephen Fox-Strangways
1865	Peter McNeil	4th Earl of Ilchester – William Thomas Horner Fox-Strangways
1889	Alfred Dight	5th Earl of Ilchester – Henry Edward Fox-Strangways
1892	Joseph Benbow	5th Earl of Ilchester – Henry Edward Fox-Strangways
1909	Joseph Benbow and Mr Kempshaw	6th Earl of Ilchester – Giles Stephen Holland Fox-Strangways (the Old Earl)
1935	Alan Lewington	6th Earl of Ilchester – Giles Stephen Holland Fox-Strangways
1960?	Alan Lewington	7th Earl of Ilchester – Edward Henry Charles James Fox-Strangways
1964	John Hussey	Lady Teresa Jane Fox-Strangways, Viscountess Galway
1979	John Kelly	Lady Teresa Jane Agnew (remarried)
1988	Reg Trevett	Lady Teresa Jane Agnew and the Honourable Charlotte Anne Morrison
1990	Stephen Griffith	The Honourable Charlotte Anne Morrison

History of the Earls of Ilchester/ Fox-Strangways Family and their Horticultural Connections

To make any sense of the family's extensive ancestry I have described the two dynasties' histories individually. Hopefully this explains some of the complexities and background of their importance in British history. I have also tried to highlight their more significant horticultural connections.

The Fox-Strangways family crest and motto ('To do without saying').

The Start of the Fox-Strangways Alliance

Susannah Strangways was married to Thomas Horner. Susannah was sole heiress to her family's West Country estates after the last male (her father, Colonel Thomas Strangways) died in 1726. The estate included the family manor Melbury House and Abbotsbury. To secure continuity of the estate she arranged a secret marriage between her 13-year-old daughter Elizabeth and Stephen Fox (Lord Ilchester and Stavordale). Joanna Martin writes in *Wives and Daughters* (2004):

> On March 15th, 1735, the marriage took place that united two great family dynasties. It was no ordinary romance in the traditional sense, for there was some clever manoeuvring behind the scenes that led to this unconventional marriage.

Although Stephen's motives for marriage may have been somewhat 'financial' and the age gap between them was 18 years, Elizabeth was a loving wife. Their marriage prospered and they had nine children. Thomas Hardy fictionalised the story of the 1st Earl and Countess of Ilchester in *A Group of Noble Dames* (1891). Hardy's family home was at Higher Bockhampton near Stinsford. The Fox-Strangways family also had one of their smaller Dorset homes, Stinsford House, built at Stinsford for their eldest daughter Susannah and her husband William O'Brien. Hardy spent a great deal of time at Stinsford House, so much so that Stinsford appears in novels and poems under the fictional name of Melstock. His ancestors had a closer connection to the Ilchester family as they had been tenants and employees of Melbury House Estate.

In 1756 Stephen Fox was created the 1st Earl of Ilchester which raised the Fox-Strangways family from landed gentry to aristocracy. He assumed the additional surname of Strangways on inheriting Melbury and the West Country Estates after the death of his mother-in-law Susannah in 1758.

The Fox Family

The Fox side of the family originally came from Farley in Wiltshire. William Fox was a wealthy yeoman farmer who married Elizabeth Pavey, daughter of Thomas Pavey of Plaitford in Wiltshire. They had two surviving sons, John and Stephen. The eldest son, John, took up arms for King Charles I and later for Charles II. He retired to France where he lived until the restoration of King Charles, when he returned to England to take up the position of clerk of the Acatry to the King's household. Stephen also joined the Royal household and in time went on to become a famous politician and financial entrepreneur. It is from Stephen's side of the Fox family that the ancestors of the Earls of Ilchester take their name.

The Rt Hon Sir Stephen Fox (1627–1716)

Stephen started work at age 15 in the household of the 10th Earl of Northumberland Algernon Percy and later for his brother Lord Percy. After 1654 he became manager to the Royal household when he fled with Charles II to the continent. The skills he gained managing the exiled King's finances abroad earned him further promotion. In November 1661 he became an MP for Salisbury, was knighted in 1665, and later became Paymaster of the Army until 1680, Lord of the Treasury, and was boss of diarist Samuel Pepys. Fox was a financial entrepreneur who put his money to good use acquiring property and

Sir Stephen Fox. Oil on canvas by John James Baker. (Courtesy of Royal Hospital Chelsea.)

building churches, alms-houses and charity schools. He was commissioned by Charles II to secure funds that led to the founding of the Royal Chelsea Hospital in 1681.

Sir Stephen acted as financial advisor in both an official and private capacity for Anne, Duchess of Buccleuch, later Duchess of Monmouth when she married the Duke of Monmouth in 1663. Incidentally, the oldest Camellias growing in Abbotsbury Gardens are called *Camellia japonica* 'Duchess of Buccleuch'. The Duke and Duchess held estates at Chiswick and may have been close neighbours to Sir Stephen. The Duke was of course the ill-fated Duke of Monmouth, the illegitimate son of King Charles II who challenged the throne of his predecessor James II. Monmouth landed his troops on a beach near the Cobb at Lyme Regis on 11 June 1685. After several skirmishes his men were forced back by Royal troops at Bridport, commanded by General Thomas Strangways, who we will hear more of later. The two forces finally met on 6 July at Sedgemoor in Somerset and the rebels were soundly beaten. This was famously known as the Monmouth Rebellion, for which the Duke paid dearly when his head was chopped off at Tower Hill, London. The Duchess of Monmouth later married the 3rd Lord Cornwallis, widower of Sir Stephen's daughter Elizabeth. James II later offered Sir Stephen a peerage on condition he converted to the Roman Catholic Church; this he refused.

Sir Stephen lived at Moreton Hall in London, which he had built between 1682 and 1684 as a three-story house with garrets next to Chiswick House. He took a keen interest in gardening and created walled kitchen gardens for his property in 1683. Daniel Defoe, author of *Robinson Crusoe*, wrote in 1725 that the house is 'the Flower of all private Gentlemen's Palaces in England'. Even William III on a private visit as he sat on the terrace overlooking the gardens announced, 'This place is perfectly fine, I could live here for five days'. The walled garden was bought by the 6th Duke of Devonshire in 1812 when Moreton Hall was demolished and the garden added to that of Chiswick House.

He was twice married (1651 and 1703); with his first wife Elizabeth Whittle he had three children, Jane, Charles and Elizabeth. From his second marriage at the age of 77 to Christiana Hope he had two sons to carry on the family name, Henry and Stephen, and two daughters, Charlotte and Christiana. Charlotte married Edward Digby in 1729, son of the 5th Lord Digby, forging an important union between these two Dorset dynasties.

Henry Fox, 1st Baron Holland of Foxley (1705–1774)

Younger son Henry worked as Secretary of War, becoming a protégé and devoted supporter of Sir Robert Walpole, long-standing Prime Minister. Henry was a regular visitor to his elder brother Stephen's house at Redlynch near Bruton in Somerset. Here he met Elizabeth Strangways, whose sister Susannah had just inherited Melbury Estate, the Strangways' family home in Dorset, in 1726. Elizabeth went on to marry James, the 5th Duke of Hamilton and Brandon, in 1727. Henry became a trusted friend of Elizabeth and was appointed as one of her trustees of part of the Melbury Estate in October 1729.

In 1742 Henry leased Holland House in Kensington and later bought it. He eloped with and married Georgina Caroline Lennox in 1744, whom he was 18 years her senior. She was the daughter of the 2nd Duke of Richmond and Lady Sarah Cadogan and a descendant of Charles II.

In 1762 George III raised Georgiana Caroline to the peerage as Baroness Holland of Holland, and less than a year later Henry became Baron Holland of Foxley for his important role in helping with the Treaty of Paris in 1763, marking the end of the Seven Year War with France and Spain. Henry was also commemorated by the great Surveyor General Samuel Holland when he named several places around Prince Edward Island in Canada (for example, there is Foxley Cove, Holland Harbour and Foxley River). Moreover, his brother Stephen Fox, the 1st Earl of Ilchester, is commemorated on the Island with place names Stavordale Cove, Ilchester Creek and Fox Cove.

Painting of Holland House by Lady Mary Ilchester, 5th Countess of Ilchester.

Henry's home at Holland House became a political and social gathering place for many famous people of the day. Henry and Georgina Caroline had three sons, Stephen, Henry Edward and Charles James. Several generations later in 1874, the Holland House estate came into the ownership of a cousin, the 5th Earl of Ilchester, a descendant of Henry's brother Stephen. It still plays an important part in Ilchester Estates' property portfolio today.

The Earls of Ilchester's Dorset properties are well represented in London in the names Abbotsbury Road, Melbury Road and Ilchester Place.

Stephen Fox, 2nd Baron Holland of Foxley (1745–1774)

Stephen was Henry Fox's eldest son. He married Lady Mary Fitzpatrick and they had one son, Henry Richard Vassall Fox, the 3rd Baron Holland, who became another major figure in British politics. Henry's wife Elizabeth Vassall (formerly married to Sir Geoffrey Webster) was a formidable woman and hosted the elite of Whig society. Her horticultural claim to fame was that she procured three species of Dahlia whilst visiting L'Abbé Cavanilles at the Madrid Royal Gardens, who in turn had them sent from Mexico. Most modern Dahlias have developed from these three original specimens: *Dahlia pinnata*, *Dahlia coccinea* and *Dahlia rosea*.

The Rt Hon Charles James Fox (1749–1806)

The middle son, Charles Fox, became a prominent Whig statesman during the reign of George III, noted for his support of the American and French Revolutions, and absolution of slavery, and famously as an arch-rival of William Pitt the Younger (the youngest Prime Minister aged 24 in 1873). Fox and Pitt were legendary oratorical and political opponents. Charles's private life was also notorious, with his love of gambling and womanising. The Fox Club is one of the first gentlemen's clubs, established in London in 1790, and still holds an annual event to celebrate his birthday. A new Fox Poker Club opened in September 2010 in Shaftesbury Avenue. Although less well known as Pitt, the word 'Whig' gave way to 'Foxite' as the self-description of members of the opposition to Pitt. A statue of his rotund figure is in Bloomsbury Square. Even to this day his name lives on as country folk nicknamed the wild fox 'Mr Charlie'.

General Hon Henry Edward Fox (1755–1811) and son Henry Stephen Fox (1791–1846)

The youngest son, Henry Edward, fought in the American War of Independence, and later became a British army general and served as Governor of Menorca.

His son Henry Stephen became His Majesty George IV's Envoy Extraordinary to the United States and a prominent botanical collector. He joined James Tweedie, former Head Botanist at the Edinburgh Botanical Gardens, on an extended trip along the coasts of Brazil and Uruguay, where they discovered several new species of Verbena (annual and perennial herbaceous or semi-woody flowering plants, the majority native to the

Americas and Europe). Incidentally, Tweedie introduced the Pampas grass *Cortadeira selloana* to Victorian Britain.

Stephen Fox, 1st Earl of Ilchester (1704–1776)

Stephen was the elder son by the second marriage of the Rt Hon Sir Stephen Fox and Christiana Hope. He was elected to the House of Commons for Shaftesbury in 1726, a seat he held until 1741, and in 1747 was created Lord Ilchester and Stavordale, Baron of Redlynch, and in 1756 1st Earl of Ilchester. He married Elizabeth Strangways-Horner, the daughter of Thomas Strangways-Horner and Susannah Strangways, in 1735. The marriage was arranged by his brother Henry and Elizabeth's mother Susannah Strangways-Horner. It served two purposes: first, as mentioned earlier, to secure the longevity of the Strangways Estate, and second, to avert an ongoing scandalous relationship that Stephen was having with his acknowledged lover Lord Hervey. Initially Lord Hervey favoured Stephen's brother Henry, who eventually and charmingly rebuffed him. From the essays *Gay History and Literature* by Rictor Norton it appears Lord Hervey himself helped steer Stephen towards this marriage. At first the marriage was merely a formal bond, the couple not living together until 1739. Thereafter they went on to enjoy a loving marriage and produced nine children.

Stephen Fox Strangways, 1st Earl of Ilchester. Pastel by Francis Coates 1748. (Courtesy of the owner and Neil Jeffares.)

In 1758 Stephen assumed the additional surname of Strangways and in 1763 he was admitted to the Privy Council. He died in September 1776, aged 72, and was succeeded by his eldest son Henry Thomas Fox-Strangways.

The Strangways Family

The Strangways family has long been associated as landed gentry, with property and estates in Dorset for hundreds of years. To cover the entire family tree in this book would be a monumental task and one that would need scholarly and detailed research. However, to get a basic understanding of their story one might start with their northern roots.

Henry Strangways was born in 1355 at South House, Yorkshire, in the time of Richard I. He had 11 children; two of his boys, Thomas and James, became the first line of Knights in the family. Thomas's home was Harlesley Castle near Northallerton.

Their younger brother Roger had a son also called Thomas. He was born in 1430 and his family lived in Strangways, a hamlet in the parish of Cheetham near Manchester. It was he who was brought to Dorset by Thomas de Grey to endow mass at the Abbey at Abbotsbury. Thomas de Grey was the 1st Marquis of Dorset, a stepson of Edward IV and a most influential personage, known as 'The Grey Marquis'.

Further down the line of descendants, another Henry Strangways bought Melbury House from William Brouning in 1500, later marrying William's widow. This has become the family seat ever since. Henry died on 14 September 1544 at the Siege of Boulogne.

Henry's son Sir Giles Strangways (1528–1562) was legally trained and became Esquire of the Body (personal attendant and courtier) to the new king Henry VIII; in fact he spent most of his life in the service of the Crown. He fought in several campaigns in France, the first in 1514 after which he was knighted, and then again in 1544. He was present at the 'Field of Cloth of Gold' in 1520. He was appointed commissioner for the dissolution of the monastery at Abbotsbury, and in 1541 he leased the abbey lands provided that 'all edifices being within the site be hereafter thrown down and removed' in accordance with Henry VIII's dissolution. After this he was granted the site of the recently dissolved monastery at Abbotsbury and the manors of Abbotsbury and East Elworth, near Portesham, for which he paid £1,906 in 1543/44. The Abbotsbury monastery site also had sentimental value as Giles's father and grandparents had been buried in the monastery's Lady Chapel. He married Joan Wadham (1533–1603) who is buried at Bristol Cathedral. They had three boys – John, James and Wadham (see below) – and two girls.

Sir John Strangways (1585–1666), his son Colonel Giles Strangways (1615–1675) and brother Colonel James Strangways

Eldest son Sir John Strangways was a politician and staunch Royalist during the English Civil War (1642–1651), which was quite a turnaround as he was once opposed to Charles I who imprisoned him in 1627. Together with his son Giles and brother James they held Abbotsbury for the King during the Civil War.

Sir John's home was the manor house in Abbotsbury where there was a fierce battle between Royalist and Parliamentary troops. Sir John and his son Giles were eventually caught at Sherborne Castle,

Sir John Strangways. (Painting at Wadham College, Oxford, by John Michael Wright.)

detained in the Tower of London by Cromwell for more than three years and had all their assets seized. In 1650 Sir John and his son Sir Giles were released, only to be kept under house arrest at Melbury. Once he had settled up by paying a large fine, his estates were returned. Giles's brother James escaped to France. Much of this story is taken from accounts by the historian Coker, author of *Coker's Survey of Dorsetshire* (1732). Cavalier Giles Strangways was elected to represent Dorset in Parliament in 1661.

A fateful piece of history was to unfold at the beginning of the Monmouth Rebellion, as previously mentioned, in which the Strangways played their part. Supporters of the Duke of Monmouth gathered under the command of Lord Grey, Colonel

Colonel Giles Strangways, Privy Councillor to Charles II. (Courtesy of Ilchester Estates.)

Wade and Captain Goodenough with a force of 400 men to advance on the Dorset Militia at Bridport. They came across the Red and Yellow Regiments commanded by Colonel James Strangways and Sir William Portman. Monmouth's forces advanced down East Street where they came under fire from the Bull Inn. Shots were fired and Wadham Strangways, Captain of Portland, was killed. Lord Grey ordered a retreat and sped back to Lyme Regis, leaving a small force to camp out at Allington in case of a counter-attack. One local well-known supporter of Monmouth was Daniel Defoe.

Colonel Thomas Strangways (1683–1726)

Col Thomas Strangways lived at the family home of Melbury House, which he altered and extended in 1692. He was the leading loyalist commoner in the county and classed as a churchman and Tory in 1708. He was the Bridport recorder in 1707 and a common councilman in 1708. On 10 February 1710 he was admitted to the Board of Brothers, a club with high Tory and Jacobite leanings. Thomas succeeded his father Colonel Thomas Strangways as Knight of the Shire for Dorset at the 1713 elections, moving to higher esteem by being promoted to High Steward in 1714. He wrote in October 1708:

> *Parliament will in short draw me and the other Tories to London where they may prevent mischief. I should have been content to turn into a downright country squire with a good pack of hounds, a smart gun, and now and then an un-godly jug of 'October' with an innocent neighbour who understands as little as myself, and spend the remainder of my days.*

October was in reference to strong ale that was brewed in October. Thomas continued to represent Dorset until his death at Melbury on 23 September 1726. Thomas had two daughters, Susannah and Elizabeth.

Elizabeth Strangways (?–1729)

Thomas's second daughter Elizabeth married James Hamilton, 5th Duke of Hamilton.

Susannah Strangways-Horner (1690–1758)

Thomas's first daughter Susannah was born at Melbury in 1690. She married Thomas Horner of Mells Park in Somerset in 1712. There is an interesting story to this name in the nursery rhyme *Little Jack Horner*. According to early

16th-century scripture, Richard Whiting, the last Abbot of Glastonbury, in order to appease Henry VIII during the dissolution sent his steward Jack Horner to London with a pie as a Christmas gift. Hidden inside were the deeds to twelve manors. Jack Horner removed the deeds to the Manor of Mells. In the 18th century this story was being attributed to Thomas Horner, Steward to Richard Whiting. This story first came into print in 1764 and the book is now in the British Museum, although there is no proof of its origin; however, highwaymen were a constant threat and many valuables were hidden in odd places so there may be some truth in it.

Little Jack Horner sat in the corner, eating his Christmas pie. He put in his thumb and pulled out a plum and said 'What a good boy am I!'

The plum was the best of the Manors.

In 1726 Susannah inherited Melbury House and Ilchester Estates on her father's death. At this time the village of Abbotsbury had a somewhat derogatory reputation. Quoting the *London Journal*: 'All the people of Abbotsbury, including the vicar, are thieves, smugglers, and plunderers of wrecks.' This rather isolated village had no school or amenities; however, changes were put in motion by Susannah, who was a generous benefactress. She donated silver plate to numerous local churches and in 1742 gave £50 for the repair of St Catherine's Chapel. Even after her death in 1758 her generosity continued to benefit the local community. According to the 'Abstract of returns of charitable Donations' at Melbury Osmond (document held in the Dorset History Centre), Susannah Strangways-Horner, by will of 28 February 1754, gave a house and garden, and rent charge of £15 payable out of Melbury Osmond annually for the instruction of poor children of the parish: vested in the Earl of Ilchester. It also stated that she gave an annuity payable out of the Manor of Abbotsbury, with a school house and £20 salary per annum.

Susannah and Thomas had two children: Elizabeth, and Thomas who died in infancy.

Elizabeth Fox-Strangways, 1st Countess of Ilchester (1722–1792)

As the family's historical background unfolds, we at last come to the most important lady of them all, as she instigated the building of Strangways

Elizabeth Fox-Strangways, 1st Countess of Ilchester. Pastel by Frances Coates 1748. (Courtesy of the owner and Neil Jeffares.)

(Abbotsbury) Castle and its walled gardens, which we know as Abbotsbury Subtropical Gardens today.

Elizabeth Fox-Strangways (née Strangways-Horner) was born in 1722. She married Stephen Fox in 1735 and, as described, this was an unusual marriage to say the least. In 1758, on the death of her mother, Elizabeth inherited the Strangways Estate and Stephen legally changed their name to Fox-Strangways. The family seat was at Melbury, along with strong family connections and interests at Abbotsbury. An oil painting of a youthful Elizabeth hangs in the hallway at Melbury House.

From her accession the family appears to have taken a much keener interest in the Abbotsbury Estate. A school was founded through the legacy provided in Susannah's will. Also a very fine large-scale map of the Estate was completed by Samuel Donne in 1758.

During the 1760s Elizabeth had a summer residence built on a bluff above Buller's Clift. The site was already in use as a cannon emplacement looking out over Lyme Bay. A walled garden was created in a sheltered area away from the Castle; known as Castle Gardens, in time this became Abbotsbury

Gothic Revival-style Abbotsbury Castle in 1765. Drawing by Samuel Grimm.

Subtropical Gardens. The new residence was often attributed specifically to Elizabeth in writings about Abbotsbury. Author C.H. Grey quotes the then Lord Ilchester as saying that 'the first Lady Ilchester built Abbotsbury Castle, by tradition out of her pin money'.

Many of these large houses were very grand but often quite atmospherically damp. This may not have helped Elizabeth, as she became quite crippled with rheumatism and spent time in Bath where she was treated for a painful hip.

By the end of the 18th century, Dorset's coastal defences played a key role amidst renewed threats of invasion from the French. Prime Minister William Pitt declared war on France in 1793 and times became increasingly difficult. This was the fifth war with France in a century. Volunteer forces were raised to complement the militia and in 1794 the Dorset Volunteer Rangers were formed. When Napoleon threatened seaborne invasion in 1798, wealthy coastal and southern-dwelling families packed up and fled to the safety of their London houses. For most of the ordinary country folk, it was business as usual.

Elizabeth and the 1st Earl of Ilchester had the following children:

- Charlotte Elizabeth (1744–1755)
- Juliana Judith (1746–1749)
- Henry Thomas, 2nd Earl of Ilchester (1747–1802): see below
- Christiana Caroline Henrietta (1750–1815)
- Stephen (1751–1836): Lt Col
- Charles (1761–1836): Rev Hon, rector at Maiden Newton from 1787
- Frances Muriel (1777–1814): married Valentine Richard Quin, 1st Earl of Dunraven and Mount-Earl, and became Baroness Adare
- Lucy (?–1787): married Colonel Hon Stephen Digby in 1771. He was courtier to George III whom he nursed through illness when the King stayed at Weymouth. He was appointed Queen Charlotte's Vice Chamberlain in 1782. His family home was Sherborne Castle

The Fox-Strangways Family

Lady Susanna Sarah Louisa Fox-Strangways (1743–1827)

Lady Susanna was known as Susan and was the eldest child of Elizabeth and Stephen. In 1764 she caused quite a scandal by eloping and marrying the actor William O'Brien against the family's wishes. William was a descendant of the Irish Earls of Clare. He gave up acting as they were forced to live in America for marrying without consent. David Garrick (actor, playwright and manager of Drury Lane) wrote in a letter:

O'Brien said that their passage of thirty four days had been a serious affair, worse than any tempest in the theatre, and he began to say short prayers. Lady Susan had been vastly ill the whole way, but was now quite well again.

Prior to their marriage William had been engaged by Garrick to appear at Drury Lane performing a new play in 1758 called *The Recruiting Officer* by George Farquhar. William continued to write at least two plays – *Cross Purposes* (1772) and *The Duel* (1773).

In 1768 he became Secretary and Provost Master General of the Bermudas. Shortly after, Lady Susanna's family forgave them and offered them a country mansion to live in at Stinsford near Dorchester. William later became Receiver General for Dorset. *The Journal of Mary Frampton* (1885) quoted: 'No two people were more liked, or their society more courted. They were most affectionately attached to each other and both lived to a reasonable advanced age.' Their vault in Stinsford church later influenced Thomas Hardy's romantic writings at an early age.

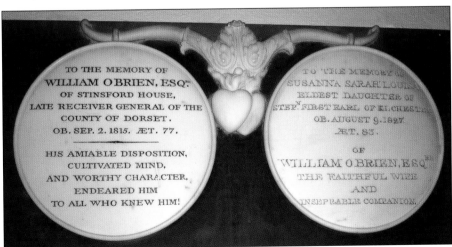

Memorial plaque to William and Lady Susanna in Stinsford church.

According to research in 1991 at the Institute of Advanced Architectural Studies in the University of York, Susan E. Schnare, a doctoral student doing a thesis on the history of Rock Gardens, came across details about Lady

Susanna O'Brien. She stated that Susanna was a keen gardener herself and designed and built one of the first rock gardens for her mother at Abbotsbury Castle. It was amongst the rocks near the sea and had four stone pavilions in the corners. She wrote a diary in which she describes the garden; however, it has yet to be found in family archives and may have perished when the family home at Abbotsbury Castle burnt down in 1913. Early pictures of the Castle do reveal the pavilions.

Henry Thomas Fox-Strangways, 2nd Earl of Ilchester (1747–1802)

Henry, the eldest son, was known as Lord Stavordale after his father became Earl of Ilchester in 1756. In 1768 he and cousin Charles James Fox were

elected members of parliament for Midhurst in Sussex. It seems politics did not dominate his life as he was more interested in shooting and hunting on his family's West Country Estates. Gambling was also a passion of his, along with his cousins Charles James and Stephen Fox. The temptations of London society were interrupted when in May 1770 he joined the 1st Regiment of Horse stationed in Ireland and then was promoted to Captain in the 24th Foot Regiment. Here he fell in love with Mary Theresa O'Grady, daughter of Standish O'Grady of Cappercullen.

They married on 26 August 1772 at Cappercullen and had eight children. Two died in infancy and the others all appear to have 'married well' into other landed gentry families, many of which had strong horticultural connections. Their home was Redlynch Park *c*

Henry Thomas Fox-Strangways, 2nd Earl of Ilchester. (Painting by Thomas Beach (Milton Abbas 1738 – Dorchester 1806), National Trust Inventory Number 996307. Courtesy of National Portrait Gallery.)

1775–1792 (previously Henry's father's estate). Mary died in 1790 and their eldest son Henry Stephen Fox-Strangways became the 3rd Earl of Ilchester.

Henry Thomas's second marriage was to Maria Digby in 1794. They had three boys. William Fox-Strangways, the eldest son from this marriage, later became the 4th Earl of Ilchester. Henry appears to have suffered reoccurring attacks of gout, a form of arthritis, in his hands and feet. In the last years of his life he was carried around in a sedan chair when he was unable to walk. He died in 1802 at Buxton, Derbyshire. It was said his death was due to 'Gout in the Head'.

Lady Christiana Caroline Henrietta Fox-Strangways (1750–1815)

Christiana was a nurse and diarist who became quite famous in her day as a heroine during the American War of Independence. She married Colonel John Dyke Acland who was a major in the 20th Foot Regiment fighting in the American War. Lady Christiana was also known as Lady Harriet according to the peerage and *Dictionary of National Biography*. Unwilling to be left behind in England, she sailed to join her husband with her mother, a valet, lady's maid and dog. Obviously Lady Harriet was no ordinary camp wife; as she followed her husband's expeditions she kept a detailed diary recording her impressions of the American landscape and native customs, which was later published.

Lady Harriet is best remembered today for her role in a far more dramatic event. In October 1777 Colonel Acland was badly wounded and taken prisoner by the Americans at the Second Battle of Saratoga (Bemis Heights). At once the pregnant Lady Harriet decided to go to him. Accompanied by her maid, a military chaplain and Acland's valet, she crossed the Hudson River in an open boat, making her way into enemy territory. While there are varying accounts of her night-time crossing, all agree that she was treated courteously by American General Horatio Gates and permitted to join her husband in captivity to nurse him. The Aclands were released and allowed to return to England (and to their daughter Kitty) in January 1778, with Lady Harriet still nursing her convalescing husband. Their son John was born on the voyage. After such perilous adventure, Lady Harriet and Colonel Acland deserved a long and happy life together at their home Pixton Park near Dulverton in Somerset. Unfortunately, Colonel Acland died later in 1778 from complications after a duel fought in defence of the American cause. The dramatic story of Lady Harriet's courage and loyalty made her a much-

Lady Acland crossing the American lines to nurse her husband, 1777. (Contemporary print by Robert Pollard, National Trust/Sophia Farley.)

praised heroine in England. The artist Robert Pollard painted his version of her river crossing, which he later turned into a popular print.

Daughter Kitty married Henry George Herbert, the 2nd Earl of Carnarvon, in 1796. Their son, the 3rd Earl, is responsible for building the family's country house Highclere Castle near Newbury, the grand house that stars in the TV series *Downton Abbey*. The Pixton Park estate remained in the Herbert family throughout the 19th century. Novelist Evelyn Waugh married Laura Herbert and their son Auberon was born at Pixton Park in 1939. Lady Harriet's father-in-law Sir Thomas Dyke Acland built a new house in 1778 at Killerton near Exeter. He employed a Scottish Head Gardener, John Veitch, who eventually became Head Steward or Agent for the estate. He later went on to establish one of the greatest plant nurseries trading in the West Country and in London. Killerton House, park and gardens are now owned by the National Trust and are open to the public.

Children of the 2nd Earl of Ilchester and his First Wife

The importance of the 2nd Earl's children and the families that they married into cannot be overlooked, as some of them were to be a great influence with horticultural interests, gardens and property. There were eleven children in all from the Earl's two marriages, but for the sake of reducing the narrative only his children with connections to Abbotsbury Gardens or horticultural interests will be mentioned.

Elizabeth Theresa Fox-Strangways (1773–1846)

Elizabeth was the 2nd Earl's eldest child. She was a well-educated woman, interested in politics and fluent in French, Latin and Greek. In 1796 she married William Davenport Talbot, an army officer who owned Lacock Abbey in Wiltshire, and they had a son, William Henry Fox Talbot (known as Henry), born on 11 February 1800 at Melbury. William died when Henry was only 5 months old, leaving Elizabeth and the estate in debt. Her family owned a number of properties, where they would live at different times. Her skilful management of the Estate restored it to a financially healthy position. Elizabeth remarried Captain Charles Fielding (Later Rear-Admiral) who became a devoted step-father to Henry. They later had two daughters, half-sisters to Henry.

Lady Mary Lucy Fox-Strangways (1776–1855)

Mary was born at Redlynch on 11 February 1776. In her mid-teens she showed great interest in chemistry and natural history and was particularly interested in plants and gardens. Her family began to regard her as an authority on horticultural matters. In 1792 the Earl took her and her brother Henry on a road trip to visit relatives in Ireland, calling in on the way to see his friend Thomas Mansel Talbot at Penrice Castle on the Gower, South Wales. Their carriage was damaged on the bumpy roads and had to be repaired and the Earl also suffered a bout of gout, which delayed their

The family church adjoining Melbury House.

journey. Mary stayed at Penrice between January and February and was enamoured with the building and its gardens. Although Thomas was almost 30 years older than Mary they fell in love and eventually married in 1794 in the Fox-Strangways' small Melbury Estate church.

They went on to have seven daughters and one son. A frequent visitor was Mary's older sister Elizabeth, who married Thomas's cousin William Davenport Talbot 2 years later. The Mansel family had held Penrice for over 300 years, with increasing wealth and economic and political strength, making them one of the most powerful families in West Glamorgan. In the late 18th century Thomas demolished his family's ancient mansion at Margam, Port Talbot in favour of the new house at Penrice on the Gower estate, but it was not until the coming-of-age of their son Christopher Rice Mansel Talbot that plans for a new house at Margam saw fruition. The original pleasure grounds remain as a country park, along with the superb Georgian Orangery that Thomas had built between 1787 and 1790.

The Orangery at Margam is said to be the longest and best preserved in Britain and the finest building of its period in the whole of Wales.

The new mansion at Margam was built in 1830 and its design was greatly influenced by the 19th-century fashionable interest in Gothic romance and medieval pageantry which lasted for so much of Victoria's reign. Christopher also drew on the stately architecture of two of the family's homes: Lacock Abbey in Wiltshire, ancestral home of the Talbots and his cousin William Henry Fox Talbot; and Melbury House in Dorset, the seat of his mother's family, the Earls of Ilchester.

Margam House, Port Talbot, Wales.

Melbury House, Melbury Sampford, Dorset.

Lady Harriet Fox-Strangways (1778–1844)

Lady Harriet married James Frampton in 1799. They lived in Moreton Hall near Dorchester, built by James's father in 1744. He gained notoriety when, as High Sheriff of Dorset, he arrested the Tolpuddle Martyrs and resurrected an old marine statute in order to have them transported to Australia. He had overreacted to incidents of barn burning and machine wrecking for fear of another indiscriminate bloodbath as with the French Revolution of 1789. Most of the Martyrs eventually returned to England and descendants of them and of the Framptons still live in the area today.

Lady Charlotte Anne Fox-Strangways (1784–1826)

Charlotte married Sir Charles Lemon, the 2nd Baronet Lemon of Carclew, at Melbury in 1810. They had three children, all of whom tragically died young. Sir Charles was an MP for Penryn in Cornwall. He served as President of the Royal Geological Society of Cornwall (1840–1856), President of the Falmouth Board of Guardians until 1837, and President of the Royal Cornwall Polytechnic Society. Their family home was Carclew House near Mylar. It was built in the fashionable Palladian style. Sir Charles was a keen horticulturalist and sponsored Sir Joseph Hooker on many of his botanising trips. This led him to be one of the first people in Britain to obtain *Rhododendron* seed from Hooker's Himalayan expedition of 1848–1850. One *Rhododendron arboreum* planted at Carclew in 1850 was recorded as being 35 ft tall by 1928. Sir Charles was a friend to Augustus Smith who was developing his great plant collection at Tresco Abbey on the Isles of Scilly. He helped introduce Augustus to Sir William Hooker, Joseph's father and the director of Kew Gardens. A hybrid Rhododendron was named 'Sir Charles

Lemon' and a recent introduction grows in Abbotsbury Gardens today. The name Lemon also lives on in Truro as Lemon Street and Lemon Quay.

Lady Louise Emma Fox-Strangways (1785–1851)

Louise married Henry Petty-Fitzmaurice in 1808 at the family church at Melbury. He was also known as Lord Henry Petty (1784–1809) and then as Earl of Kerry until 1818. He later became the 3rd Marquess of Lansdowne, and as a result of this marriage Lady Louise became known as the Marchioness of Lansdowne. Henry was a most powerful Whig statesman and notably served as Home Secretary and Chancellor of the Exchequer. He was frequently consulted by Queen Victoria on matters of importance. Lady Louise held the office of Lady of the Bedchamber between the years 1837 and 1838. Their home was Bowood House, which had been in Lord Lansdowne's family for generations and was one of the finest properties in Wiltshire. The house included a magnificent orangery and the grounds were landscaped by Capability Brown in the 1760s, who incorporated a large lake and arboretum of rare trees. Henry also commissioned the great Italianate terraced gardens on the south front of the house.

Henry Stephen Fox-Strangways, 3rd Earl of Ilchester and Lord Stavordale (1787–1858)

Henry was the eldest son and became the 3rd Earl of Ilchester in 1802. In 1835 he was appointed Captain of the Yeomen of the Guard and made Privy Councillor in 1837. Being a British peer and Whig politician he was a busy man but still found time to run his Dorset estate. It was he who initiated the planting of much of the woodland around Abbotsbury after the Enclosure Acts enabled parcels of land to be joined up for more efficient husbandry. The woodland surrounding the Gardens is still known today as Stavordale Wood and many of the older Oak trees would have been planted at this time. He was appointed Lord Lieutenant of Somerset in 1837 and made Lieutenant-Colonel Commandant of the Dorsetshire Yeomanry in 1846. He married Caroline Leonora Murray in 1812. She died giving birth to their fourth child in 1819. Their children were Henry Thomas Leopold, Theresa Anna Maria (who married Edward Digby), Stephen and Caroline Margaret. Henry died at Melbury on 8 January 1858 aged 70. Both his sons predeceased him and he was succeeded by his half-brother William Fox-Strangways.

Caroline Augusta Fielding (1808–1881)

Caroline married Ernest Augustus Edgcumbe, the 3rd Earl of Mount Edgcumbe. Their family home was Mount Edgcumbe House set in Grade I listed Cornish Gardens within 865 acres of country park on the Rame peninsula, south-east Cornwall. They also owned Cotehele in Saltash, a medieval manor house now in the care of the National Trust. Caroline was invested with the Royal Order of Victoria and Albert, Second Class, and was known as Lady Caroline Edgcumbe. Caroline's later position as lady in waiting to the Queen strengthened her half-brother William's royal contacts.

Henrietta Horatio Maria Fielding (1810–1851)

Henrietta married Thomas Gaisford and they were close to her half-brother William and influenced him artistically.

Children of the 2nd Earl of Ilchester and his Second Wife

The 2nd Earl's second marriage to Maria Digby, his first cousin, produced three more children: William, Giles and John.

Hon William Thomas Horner Fox-Strangways, 4th Earl of Ilchester (1795–1865)

William was styled as the Honourable William Fox-Strangways until 1858. He was a British diplomat and Whig politician, a Fellow of the Royal Society and Linnean Society, and served as an attaché at the British Embassies in Naples, Florence, St Petersburg and The Hague. He succeeded his half-brother Henry to become the 4th Earl of Ilchester in 1858, the same year he entered the House of Lords.

William married Sophia Penelope Sheffield in 1857. They had no children. He had a passion for art and botany and the latter was evident through letters of correspondence he held with his half-sister Lady Mary Lucy Fox-Strangways and nephew Henry Talbot, where they often discussed what was in flower in each other's gardens. The picture gallery in Christ Church,

Left: a young William Horner Fox-Strangways, 4th Earl of Ilchester; by an unknown artist, this painting hangs in offices at Melbury House. Right: William in later life. (© National Trust/ Rachael Topham.)

Oxford, where William was educated, houses a fine collection of early Italian paintings that he donated and he also gave a further 41 paintings to the Ashmolean Museum. It was he who influenced the development of the early plant collections at Abbotsbury and archived letters between his sisters and nephew show that botanical matters or 'botanising' was a great passion of theirs.

William and Sophia's London residence was No. 31 Old Burlington Street in the parish of St James, Westminster. Their other country houses were Redlynch and, most importantly, Abbotsbury Castle. It is here that William spent most of his time when not abroad and the garden where he planted many of his rare plant introductions that he brought back from his diplomatic trips abroad. He was a well-respected landlord and philanthropist who ensured many new labourers cottages were built on the estate. William died at Melbury in January 1865 aged 69. His funeral was meant to be a private family affair, but many of his tenants attended the churchyard by horseback, the shops in the village closed in respect and all flags flew at half-mast at the coastguard station. In his will and testament he stated:

I hereby leave to my dear wife Sophia Penelope Countess of Ilchester the choice of my two country houses. The garden at Abbotsbury, if that be the residence chosen by her, is to be kept up on its present principle of an 'Experimental garden' for naturalising useful and curious trees, shrubs and other plants.

He was succeeded by his nephew Henry Edward Fox-Strangways, the 5th Earl of Ilchester.

Hon Giles Digby Robert Fox-Strangways (1798–1827)

Captain of the 7th Hussars, he died at Abbotsbury Castle aged 28 on 12 February 1827.

Hon John George Charles Fox-Strangways (1803–1859)

John was a British diplomat, a Whig politician, and served as a courtier or gentleman usher to Queen Adelaide. He was an MP for Calne in Wiltshire in 1836 and later a clerk in the Foreign Office. He married Amelia Marjoribanks in 1844 and their son Henry became the 5th Earl of Ilchester in 1865.

Henry Edward Fox-Strangways, 5th Earl of Ilchester (1847–1905)

Henry succeeded his uncle William to the earldom in 1865 and was then able to take his seat in the House of Lords on his 21st birthday. He was a British peer and Liberal politician, and at the young age of 26 was appointed Captain of the Honourable Corps of Gentlemen-at-Arms in the Liberal administration of Gladstone and admitted to the Privy Council. He also gained rank as Captain in the service of the Dorset Yeomanry Cavalry. He served as Lord Lieutenant of Dorset from 1885–1905.

The 5th Earl of Ilchester, caricatured by Spy in Vanity Fair, *1882.*

Henry married Lady Mary Eleanor Dawson, daughter of Richard Dawson, the 1st Earl of Dartrey, in 1872. He took on Holland House Estate in 1874 from a distant cousin of the Holland barony. As a mark of his standing he was caricatured by Leslie Ward in *Vanity Fair* in July 1882. Lady Mary was a renowned hostess of splendid garden parties at Holland House and was always intensely anxious to make others happy. Her own troubles and frequent ill-health were put aside. The majority of her precious letters, diaries and wonderful sketches were lost when Abbotsbury Castle was destroyed by fire in 1913.

Henry, like his predecessors, was an enthusiastic patron of Abbotsbury Church and it was with his support that they had the interior redesigned to reflect Victorian values. Lord Ilchester and Lady Mary also showed considerable devotion to Abbotsbury Gardens, enlarging them and the plant collections with the help of Head Gardener Joseph Benbow. Joseph had previously been working for Sir Thomas Hanbury whose famous home and garden was La Mortola on the French–Italian Riviera. This

Lady Mary Eleanor Dawson, 5th Countess of Ilchester. (Courtesy of Mrs Townshend.)

must surely have influenced his Mediterranean-style planting and influx of new and rare plants. So much so that in 1898 Lady Mary commissioned a hard-bound book catalogue listing the 4,000 species of plants growing in the Gardens. Sir Thomas Hanbury was famous for buying Wisley Gardens for £5,000 and gifting it to the Royal Horticultural Society in 1903. His son Sir Cecil Hanbury bought Kingston Maurward House outside Dorchester. The Earl of Ilchester also had 'title to wreck' and fishing rights and there were many disputes with local fishermen that he had to deal with. The Dorset History Centre holds a letter sent to Lord Ilchester on 22 May 1889:

My Lord,
Henry Dark and his crew were fishing opposite middle meadows early this morning and ongoing found some fish. An east country boat with Captain Moyteo went round outside them and broke Dark's seine net and pulled it up with about 700 fish in it. They assaulted the crew knocking down two or three. Please could your Lordship have these men prosecuted as all Abbotsbury fishermen feel they should not be allowed to come here. I am your Lordship's most obedient. J Hutchings

Henry Edward Fox-Strangways, 5th Earl of Ilchester, with his devoted Golden Retriever 'Ada'. (Courtesy of Mrs Townshend.)

The family have always been avid dog lovers and in the sheltered Valley Garden at Melbury there is a dogs' graveyard. The headstones are engraved with names and dates going back generations.

'Yellow retriever' was the original name of the breed, superseded by 'Golden retriever' by Lord Harcourt. Sir Dudley Coutts Marjoribanks (brother of the Hon Mrs John Fox-Strangways) was a keen breeder of dogs and from 1835 kept important stud books. One story goes that in 1868 a travelling circus sold one of their Caucasus mountain sheep dogs to Sir Dudley, and in due course the first of the yellow breed began. Stud book entries do not tie up. The Ladykirk breed of Tweed Water Spaniel crossed with retrievers, Labradors and black wavy coats started the Ilchester breed. It began with 'Nous' in 1868 and 'Ada' her daughter. All the family dogs are buried in a pets graveyard in the grounds of Melbury, including Nous and Ada.

Henry and Mary had three children:

- Giles Stephen (1874–1959): see below.
- Lady Muriel Augusta (1876–1920): married in 1903 to her second cousin once-removed Major George Hugh Digby of Chalmington, Dorchester.
- Hon Denzil Vesey (1879–1901): a small copse in Abbotsbury is still known as Denzil's Wood.

Giles Stephen Holland Fox-Strangways, 6th Earl of Ilchester (1874–1959)

Giles was a British peer and philanthropist. He became an officer in the Coldstream Guards and was decorated with the Legion of Honour and awarded an OBE in 1919. From 1922–1959 he was a trustee of the National Portrait Gallery and of the British Museum, and a member and chairman of the Royal Commission on Historical Monuments. He was President of the London Library, Royal Literary Fund and Roxburghe Club, along with being steward of the Jockey Club from 1937–1940. He was awarded a GBE in 1950 when he was invested with the Knight of the Grand Cross. A picture in the Getty digital archive collection shows him and Lady Helen, his wife, on 'Black Ascot Day', when everyone was in mourning for King Edward VII. He also held the office of Deputy Lieutenant of Dorset before 1956. He married Lady Helen Vane-Tempest Stewart, daughter of the 6th Marquess of Londonderry, in 1902. Lady Helen continued the interest in Abbotsbury Gardens and enrolled them in the National Gardens Scheme in 1927. They had four children:

- Lady Mary Theresa (1903–1948): married Captain John Herbert and became a Woman of the Bedchamber for HRH Princess Elizabeth 1944–1948.
- Edward Henry Charles James (1905–1964): see below.
- Hon John Denzil (1908–1961): like his father he joined the Coldstream Guards and rose to rank of Lieutenant. He fought in World War II and was held as a POW.
- Lady Mabel Edith (1918–1995): married Ivor Grosvenor Guest,

Lady Mary Fox-Strangways and Captain Herbert (parents of Robin Herbert, ex-President of the RHS) at Abbotsbury, 24 May 1924, with wedding gifts.

2nd Viscount Wimborne, Lieutenant in the TA Royal Tank Corps and later Liberal MP for Brecon and Radnor. She later became the Dowager Viscountess

Lady Helen, 6th Countess of Ilchester, with daughter Mabel.

Dowager Viscountess Wimborne.

Wimborne when the 2nd Viscount died in 1967. A notable gardener and stalwart member of the International Dendrology Society, she was known for introducing *Ceanothus* 'Concha'. They lived on two very different islands, Jamaica and Guernsey, and raised four children. For 25 years she was President of the Northamptonshire Red Cross.

Edward Henry Charles James Fox-Strangways, 7th Earl of Ilchester (1905–1964)

Edward was born on 1 October 1905. He succeeded to the title of 7th Lord Ilchester and Stavordale, Baron of Redlynch and 7th Earl of Ilchester on the death of his father Giles on 29 October 1959. He gained the rank of Captain in the Royal Horse Guards and in 1959 held the office of Deputy Lieutenant of Dorset. He married Helen Elizabeth Ward in 1937. Like her predecessors, she was actively involved in running the Gardens. They had three children, but the 7th Earl died in 1964 without a surviving male heir:

- Giles Henry Holland (1934–1947): died in an accident aged 13.
- Charles Stephen (1938–1958): gained the rank of 2nd Lieutenant in the Royal Horse Guards, he was killed on active service while on emergency operations in Cyprus, aged 20.
- Lady Teresa Jane (1932–1989): see below.

Lady Teresa Jane Fox-Strangways (1932–1989)

Teresa married Simon George Robert Monckton-Arundell in 1953 and was styled as Viscountess Galway. Simon, who took the title 9th Viscount Galway, was commissioned into the Life Guards in 1948, retired as a Major in 1960 and became Deputy Lieutenant for Nottinghamshire in 1963. His family were significant land owners in Nottinghamshire; their family home was Serlby Hall. He died in 1971 aged just 40. They had one daughter, the Honourable Charlotte Anne Monckton.

Lady Teresa remarried Richard Mark Walter Agnew in 1972. He gained the rank of Lieutenant in the Royal Navy and was Aide-de-Camp to the Governor of Malta from 1954–1955. Together they managed the Dorset estate and made a considerable starting contribution to the restoration of the Gardens during the 1970s and 1980s.

Hon Charlotte Anne Townshend (née Monckton) (1955–present)

Charlotte married Guy Morrison in September 1983 and divorced in 1987. They had one child, Simon George Strangways Morrison, in 1984. Her second marriage was to James Reginald Townshend in 1995. He has a strong background in Agriculture as the Chief Executive of Velcourt Farms Group plc and as the British Business Ambassador for Agriculture. They have one daughter, Melissa Susan Charlotte Townshend, born 1996.

Charlotte became a Deputy Lieutenant of Dorset in 1999 and the High Sheriff of Dorset in 2005. She is also Joint Master of the Cattistock Hunt. She inherited Ilchester Estates business and property from her mother, and large areas of West

The Honourable Charlotte Townshend.

Dorset including the Fleet, Chesil Beach, Swannery, Tithe Barn, the family home at Melbury and of course Abbotsbury Gardens. The Estate also includes much of Holland Park and the surrounding area in London.

Cattistock Hunt c 1914.

The Fox Talbot Papers and Correspondence with William Fox-Strangways, the 4th Earl of Ilchester

As mentioned, William Henry Fox Talbot (Henry Talbot) (1800–1877) was the nephew of William Fox-Strangways, the 4th Earl of Ilchester. He was a famous inventor and pioneer of photography, an MP for Chippenham (1832–1835), High Sheriff of Wiltshire (1840), and famed for his book *English Etymologies*. He was also a great letter writer, whether they were of

William Henry Fox Talbot. Photograph taken by John Moffat of Edinburgh in 1866 (© NTPL/Nick Carter).

scientific interest or to members of his family. Even at the age of 8, Henry told his stepfather to 'tell everyone I write to, to keep my letters and not burn them'. Most of the letters are held at the Fox Talbot Museum at Lacock Abbey, his family home.

He was known to have corresponded with 1,100 people, and more than 2,000 of his hand-written letters have been traced so far. There was hardly any member of the family with whom he did not correspond on botanical matters, but there was a far greater intimacy when writing to his favourite uncle William. Their correspondence showed a genuine excitement over the discovery of a new plant or new region they had visited during their travels.

The following has been sourced from *The Correspondence of William Henry Fox Talbot* (www.foxtalbot.dmu.ac.uk), an online project dedicated to collecting all associated comprehensive editions of all correspondence and transcripts to and from Talbot, amounting to over 10,000 letters. The editor and project director is Professor Larry Schaaf, with additional development and hosting by De Montfort University, Leicester.

William, like Henry, was only able to devote part of his time to botany, in his case because of his sojourns abroad as a diplomat. He often contributed to the *Gardener's Magazine* and was a Fellow of the Linnean Society. As a botanist and plant collector he was accorded the honour of having two genera named after him – a Chinese shrub/small tree called *Stransvaesia* (taken from the family name Strangways) (now known as *Photinia*) and *Foxia* (now incorporated into the genus *Hyacinthus*). The first Director of the Royal Botanic Gardens at Kew was Sir William Jackson Hooker (1785–1865). He was one of the most widely respected botanists of the age and expanded Kew Gardens and built extensive hothouses to accommodate the ever-increasing quantities of exotic new plants. A young Henry corresponded directly with William Hooker on botanical interests, often seeking help in plant identification, as did his uncle William Fox-Strangways.

The following extracts are from letters highlighting dialogue relevant to the Abbotsbury Gardens. In some cases there is talk of family visits; other letters are discussing flowering plants of interest or letters to eminent botanists of the day.

Much of William's time was spent abroad on diplomatic missions and his letters often refer to saunters into the countryside around Nice, St Petersburg and Florence. In Italy much time was spent with Joseph Giuseppe Raddi (1770–1829), a well-known Italian botanist. Talk was of wild flowers and seed or cuttings that he would send back to Henry and of the conditions of the roads and access. It was his garden at Abbotsbury that consumed William's mind, yet it seems all was in good hands. An early letter dated 24 February 1825 (Ref: 1256) reveals that he received reports from Harriot Georgina Mundy (née Frampton), William Henry Fox Talbot's cousin and sister-in-law, who tended it while he was away.

I continue to receive satisfactory reports of my garden from Ht Frampton who tends it at Abbotsbury. Everything seems at least a fortnight earlier there – besides they keep Arbutus & Cypress & 50 other hardy things in the Greenhouse here – I don't understand your metamorphosis – it would lead to the exploded doctrine of equivocal generation. I have found Euphraxia lutea *& I think C.* lanatus *in Russia flowering in the end of August – it must be on a mountain at Nice that they flower not till October. – Come & pay me a visit & see Raddi & go yrself to the Islands –*

On 2 November 1837 (Ref: 3611) William writes to Henry from Abbotsbury with lists of plants seen growing at Abbotsbury:

Not having been here since May I find a great deal new, and some deficiencies after the winter and spring. I find come up some seeds I did not expect, Pistacia vera, Cytisus ramosissimus, Mattia umbellate, Ebenus cretica, Ilex opaca, Pinus excels, Negundium americanum, Cassia nictitans, Schinus molle, Celastrus scandens, *and among the plants I find three* Salvia leucanthas *going to flower beautifully for the first time I believe in England, this comes of putting them out. Also* Bidens procera *and* longifolia, Pelargonium triste, Colchicum montanum *var* cupani, Convolvulus italicus *and* cantabrica, Delphinium intermedium, Campanula muralis, Silphium laciniatum, *and I find one or two German plants I had despaired of growing well. Also* Rosa aciphylla, Spirea decumbens, Primula rhaetica *and* elatior vera, *and 3 sorts of dwarf almond from Vienna. Some ferns too are doing well out of doors but they must take their chance for the winter –* Onoclea sensibilis, Davallia canariensis, Adiantum pedatum *and* Woodwardsia radicans. *We had tremendous gales, that of yesterday I think surpassed anything I've seen – I hope they are over. Several trees are broken in Stavordale Wood.*

Another year on, in a letter of 16 November 1838 (Ref: 3754) there is mention of a new glass house and first evidence of communications with the Caucasus (the mountainous Europe–Asian border region between the Black Sea and Caspian Sea), possibly the source of seed for the magnificent Caucasian Wingnut trees (*Pterocarya fraxinifolia*).

I meant to write to you from Abbotsbury, we had a delightful autumn altogether. I have got a volunteer communication with the Crimea and Caucasus of which I hope to avail myself; I have already got some interesting seeds and bulbs from here. Tell Horatia to look at our new house at Abbotsbury, a simple glass house with flue which cost under £60. Our great beauties at Abbotsbury this season were and still are Convolvulus cneorum *in full blow, a quantity of* Cosmeas *which are very gay,* Mesembs *of course,* Linum caespitosum *and a stock from Madeira which I take to be* Cherianthus littoreous.

Receipts found at Melbury House show plants being purchased from the Horticultural Society's Garden at Chiswick on 3 October 1839 to be dispatched by coach to Abbotsbury.

There is reference to Minterne House in a letter from William to Henry on 9 March 1851 (Ref: 6396). This was the seat of Lord Digby and thus the married home of William's cousin Theresa Digby, a daughter of the 3rd Earl of Ilchester. William says:

I found two years ago in the woods at Minterne the double pseudonarcissus, *quite different from the garden double which is evidently the double of* luteus *or* major, *and quite agreeing with its natural single wild daffodil. Poor Dr Herbert would have rejoiced in this.*

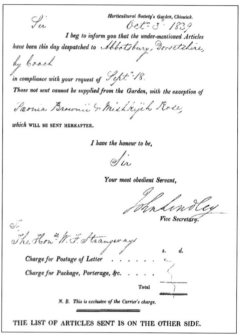

Invoice from the Horticultural Society's Garden, Chiswick, 3 October 1839. The choice Peonie plant would have travelled by horse and coach from London to Dorset.

Dr William Herbert was Dean of Manchester (1778–1847), an MP, clergyman, botanist and linguist. William was a regular customer at Loddiges nursery. At the time, this was one of the most impressive plant nurseries which specialised in introduced exotic plants, trees, shrubs, Palms, Ferns and Orchids. George Loddiges established the world's largest hothouse in

Cabbage palm, exotic plants and carefully posed children, a popular combination in the Edwardian era.

his Hackney Botanic Nursery where he created a 'tropical rainforest' to house his epiphytic orchids, ferns and Camellias. He visited Abbotsbury Gardens in 1863 when he presented William with a 'Palmetto' or 'scrub cabbage palm' from the south-eastern United States.

There are references to horticultural nursery suppliers in a letter dated 20 May 1853 (Ref: 6801) when William writes to Henry saying:

Yesterday I went to Low and Loddiges. Low has not half the plants he pretends to have in his catalogue – but he has some out of way things. Loddiges no longer sells anything except orchids – all his stock is purchased by the Crystal palace. I had luck to meet the Portuguese owner of that delightful garden at Sao Miguel, Azores, described in the Gardeners' Chronicle. *He is visiting Abbotsbury while he is in England to see what of their plants, among others, have been acclimatised.*

The original Walled Garden at Abbotsbury was built to serve as protection from the windswept coast and as a kitchen garden. In a letter dated 6 October 1857 (Ref: 407) William refers to it:

Our Grapes at Abbotsbury are as large and fine as in France and perfectly ripened, not against a wall but a reed fence – cucumbers also, sown in the open ground, and trained on espaliers, figs as usual in profusion.

In a short letter written at Melbury by William to Henry on 28 December 1859 (Ref: 8014) there is reference to meeting a party of friends at Evershot station, where a carriage was to take the party on to Melbury. They were Mr and Mrs Henry Hobhouse of Hadspen House, neighbours of William when he lived at Redlynch.

Melbury, 28 Decr

My dear Henry

I recommend you & your party to come to the Evershot Station by the 4.55. Train – a carriage shall meet you there at 5. You will find here Mr & Mrs Hobhouse, Gaisfords sister – they are neighbours of ours at Redlynch –

I had also asked Walter Strangways to come, but his Father has since been taken ill & I fear will not recover which of course will prevent him.

I hear from Kew that they have got from N. Zealand some fine grasses, equal to the so-called Pampas Grass.
A happy Xmas to all

Yr affte uncle
W^m

In some of the letters there are interesting discussions about the important news of the day, such as the first publication by John Murray in November 1857 of David Livingstone's *Missionary Travels and Researches in South Africa*, and in a letter dated 23 October 1858 (Ref: 7711) there is great excitement when William describes his first sighting of Donati's Comet.

Redlynch, 23 Oct

My dear Henry

I do not know where you are, but selon les probabilités, not where I direct to you. I have been going to write to you again & again from Abbotsbury to tell you of the beauties this fine season has called forth – but not having done so on the spot, the impression has already faded a little by absence.

You have of course been occupied with the comet, we saw it beautifully but I wish it had been more above the horizon. It is the first real looking comet I ever saw. I want to know why its tail curves like brush if it encounters no resisting motion. Is the tail a reality, or only an effect produced by its light shed upon a material, but without it, invisible æther? I hope to see some interesting reports & observations of it published during the winter with photographs.

The fine summer made everything flower magnificently & has covered the Ilexes & Bays with such crops of fruit as I never saw before – the acorns are in bunches, & bay berries clothe the branches like holly berries. Some odd varieties of oak too are bearing which I never saw before. I hope you have Crocus speciosus *– the beauty of autumnal crocuses, & the* Saffron *– sativus, which* *does so well with us, tho' at Spofforth it flowered once in 15 years. Tell me what curiosities you have had – love to Ela & Co*

Yr Aff
W^m

An eminent botanist of the day was James McNab who was director of the Royal Botanic Garden Edinburgh, with whom favours or swaps of plants were often arranged. In one letter the 4th Earl seeks a favour from Henry about sourcing a new plant, and the very fact that the Earl mentions the Oaks that he collected from North America has been a useful reference in assessing the age of some of the huge Oak trees that are still growing in the Gardens today.

Melbury, Dorchester, 27 Sept 1862 (Ref: 8853):

My dear Henry,

I suppose you are now enjoying the fine autumn there is said to be in Scotland while we are in fogs & rain without ceasing. If you visit occasionally the Botanic Garden can you learn for me if they have a rare plant called Nyctanthes Arbor tristis *which I have long desiderated – wishing to collect all the* tristes *I can. (Weeping forms)*
  I hope soon to go to Abbotsbury where I will give you some account of the vegetable worlds there. Here I am trying to get up all the Oaks of North America. Some do very well.

The following letter of 16 April 1862 (Ref: 8541) is from William to Henry, with horticultural reference to Abbotsbury and Sir William Hooker:

We are just returned from a few weeks stay at Abbotsbury, I never knew so wet a March. Never the less I never saw finer or more abundant Rhododendrons, Camellias and Narcissi – though their beauty was dimmed by the constant rains. For the first time I saw Camellia reticulata *flower and that magnificently out of doors. We have* Primula involucrate *and* Camassia esculenta *in flower; both nice plants – if you have an open day I recommend you pay Hooker a visit at Kew.*

Another garden with an historical botanical collection that grows on the island of Tresco in the Isles of Scilly, Cornwall, is Tresco Abbey Gardens.

Obtaining plants for Abbotsbury is spoken of in many letters. Here is evidence of plants coming from Tresco. The plants were from William Henry Fox Talbot's half-sister Lady Charlotte Louisa 'Charry' Traherne (née Talbot).

3 December 1863 (Ref: 8765):

Charlotte sends me plants from Isles of Scilly and Marazion, Mr Smith seems to have a botanic garden there. Habea pectinata *seems very fine there – but not in your northern climate, it is not right to tantalise you with such things. Many thanks for the Tree lupin seeds. Our gardener at Abbotsbury used to write it Turlupin seed – his other slip slop calling* Amyris polygama *calling it* Amorous polygamy, *this has left an indelible impression in my memory.*

On 6 May 1863 (Ref: 8703) Henry writes to Professor John Hutton Balfour, Scottish botanist (1808–1884), on behalf of his uncle William and thanks him for the offer of some Palm trees:

Dear Sir,

Lord Ilchester is very much obliged to you for the list of Palms. He says that he possess Chamaerops palmetto *and that none of the others would be hardy on the south coast of Dorsetshire. He is in search of the* Areca sapinda *of New Zealand which is hardy. Also of Madeira and Canary plants, those of which he has do so well in Dorset.* Campanula vidalli *for example (that however is Azorian). He cannot get an* Ardesia excels. *He proposes to send the Edinburgh Botanical garden some bulbs, at the proper season, they are in flower now. I think you would like to see his collection at Abbotsbury.*

This letter mentions other prominent people of the day and shows how William had many influential contacts in the world of botany. George Bentham (1800–1884) was a philosopher and botanist. The reference to *Hooker* was most likely Sir Joseph Dalton Hooker (1817–1911), a friend of Bentham, or possibly his father Sir William.

18 July 1864 (Ref: 8853) from William to Henry:

My dear Henry,

as soon as you were gone I had plants to show you which escaped me – Vella pseodocytisus, *with its odd little* silicules. Ferulla tingitana – *the Moroccan* ammoniac, *a handsome umbellifer.* Prium maritimum, *in flower.* Dykia remotiflora – *on the terrace and* Quercus glabra *coming into flower, the only late and pretty flowering oak. Bentham could not come, I am going to send a branch of the Aloe, with a leaf to Hooker, the bunches are now out partially nearly up to the top, very bright and yellow in the sun. The Aloe is dropping honey in profusion attracting all vagabond insects. We return to Melbury this afternoon. There has been a great thunderstorm as near as Bridport, but none here. The air was wonderfully clear one evening but ever since covered with a thin film of mist.*

Writing from William's London home at 31 Burlington Street, he mentions other family visits:

My dear Henry, I am very sorry I cannot make one of the party to Mount Edgcumbe.

Mount Edgcumbe near Plymouth was the seat of the Earl of Mount Edgcumbe who married William's half-sister Caroline Augusta Edgcumbe (née Fielding).

I am now promised to various parts of the East of England, and could only spare a few days to Lacock or Brickworth [once owned by Lord Nelson, and later William's uncle John George Fox-Strangways] *or at farthest to Abbotsbury – I have promised a visit to Carclew in the autumn when I shall hope to find Caroline still at Mt Edgcumbe.*

Carclew in Cornwall was the seat of Sir Charles Lemon and Lady Lemon, née Lady Charlotte Anne Fox-Strangways.

The Melbury Archive Papers

From recently discovered archive material held at Melbury House, more letters from these distinguished horticulturalists of their day have revealed regular communication with the 4th Earl of Ilchester. Several letters with the embossed seal of 'Royal Gardens Kew' make interesting reading.

A letter dated 26th Dec 1858 from the director of Kew Gardens, Sir William Joseph Hooker, thanks Lord Ilchester for a brace of pheasants, and goes on to note how he was always craving for more glass and was happy to be able to report commencement of a new conservatory next year, this being the famous largest surviving Victorian temperate house in the world today.

Another letter dated March 1st 1859 sent to the Earl of Ilchester is from John Smith, who was a botanist and the first curator at the Royal Botanic Gardens, Kew. He thanks Lord Ilchester for seeds of *Illicium religiosum* that he sent to Kew and explained that they would not thrive out of doors.

Interestingly, a letter sent to Lord Ilchester addressed from 1 Eaton Square, Belgravia, London, is from Augustus Smith, who was a politician and famously known for being the Governor of the Isles of Scilly, where he developed the unique subtropical garden at Tresco Abbey in the early 19th century. He thanks Lord Ilchester for the offer of some game and goes on to say how he has tried to introduce Partridge to the Islands without success. The letter mentions growing *Aralia sieboldii* which have flowered for the last three winters on Tresco, and Augustus asks, '*Could you supply me with a Sugar-cane plant in the spring? There is a species grown at Madeira, which I think might answer.*'

Sir Joseph Dalton Hooker succeeded his father Sir William Joseph Hooker as director of Kew Gardens. He was one of the greatest British botanists and explorers of the 19th century. There are many plants growing in Abbotsbury Gardens that have the taxa named in his honour – plants such as *Sarcococca hookeriana*, *Crinodendron hookerianum* and *Iris hookeri*.

A letter sent to Lord Ilchester from Joseph Hooker stamped and dated January 23rd 1862 from the Royal Gardens, Kew, reads:

My Lord,
I beg to thank you very much for the interesting list you have sent of herbaceous hardy things at Abbotsbury – it astonished me in many ways, most especially curious is the list of Australian ferns, Cyathea dealbata *and* Allantodia australis,

none of which are at all high south temperate forms, and none of which are, so far as I am aware, ever exposed in their native countries to anything like ordinary frosts of this climate. Chamaerops martiniana *ought to be more hardy than it is, but* Livistona australis *growing out of doors in England and withstanding last winter's frost, is indeed marvellous, as is* Xanthorrhoea hostillis. *I do not remember having seen either of these species in Tasmania, though the* Chamaerops *approaches the South East extreme of Australia.*

He goes on to say,

I expect a packet of Himalayan seeds soon, and if they contain anything worth sending I will put some aside for your Lordship. My father is still remarkably well though in his 77th year even, and never relaxes for a moment – he has been troubled with deafness lately, he desires his best compliments.

The Branch Experimental Garden in the South would be very charming, but the Director General would be always there, not here, in my case!!

This letter has revealed two very interesting points. One is that in the autumn of 2002 I managed to obtain a specimen of *Trachycarpus martiana*, its old name or synonym being *Chamaerops martiniana*, the very same palm tree that was mentioned by Joseph Hooker. It initially suffered winter damage for the first few years and has since grown from strength to strength in the border facing West Lawn.

The second point of interest is that in the years I have been researching this book, I really gained an insight and sense of how deeply involved and passionate the 4th Earl, Lord Ilchester, was about his garden and of his pure delight with new plant introductions, by sharing with friends and family all news of his garden at Abbotsbury. By reading in between the lines of this last letter it would appear that he was in discussion with the directors of Kew Gardens to offer Abbotsbury as an 'Experimental Garden' for the South – a garden to trial new and wondrous tender plants outside without the need for elaborate glass-house protection. What I wonder would have been the outcome if these plans had gone ahead. Would Abbotsbury have provided an early tourist boom and a mecca for all plantaholics in the 19th century?

I suspect not, as it was still very much a family home and I'm sure the next generation of the Fox Strangways family would have ensured a healthy balance between keeping the Gardens as a scientific base and for the pleasure of their own little piece of heaven. This is of course just speculation, but it is fun to ponder.

Looking to the Future

There have been many examples of great gardens lost and then restored in the last couple of decades, such as Aberglasney in Carmarthenshire and the Lost Gardens of Heligan in Cornwall. A garden is only as good as the person or people that drive it, and once change occurs, be it a death in the family, war or financial loss, a garden can very quickly fall into decline as nature takes over, infrastructure decays and dominant plant species prevail. Abbotsbury was a garden lost in time, with an 18th-century history overlaid with new ideas and planting schemes that each generation had brought to it, but with no overriding plan to refer back to. In helping to revive this once tired and neglected garden we have injected life into a green oasis. With an ambitious restoration strategy, tackling small sections at a time, slowly but surely people are sitting up and taking notice.

Abbotsbury is unique as a British garden with its distinct continental feel and ambience of a far-flung lost British outpost. There are now flowering plants that cover all seasons, where once it was known, like many Cornish gardens, as a 'Spring garden'. Garden events attract another audience throughout the year, along with improved visitor amenities, which now point to a brighter future. In 2012 the Gardens won the Historic Houses Association (HHA) Christie's Garden of the Year Award, which marks a turning point in the Gardens' long history.

We have introduced thousands of new and rare plants, with all

Receiving HHA Christie's Garden of the Year Award 2012.
From left to right: Stephen Griffith (Gardens Curator),
Edward Harley (Historic Houses Association), Charlie
Cator (Christie's) and Mrs Townshend.

sorts of combinations, whilst taking care to use bold foliage against upright linear leaves, woodland groundcover for shade, colourful perennials for summer impact and tropical architectural shapes for the subtropical effect. Some parts of the Gardens are bright, bold and clashing in colour, which may be vulgar to the classical eye but daring, cheeky and fun to the less judgemental.

There will never be a defining moment when one can stand back and say the Gardens are now restored and complete, as a garden never stands still. It is rather like 'painting the Forth Bridge'; no sooner have you planted and moved on to another project than plants, paths and edging need revisiting. Trees age and die, shrubs flower well one year and not the next, and planting schemes look fresh for a couple of years and then need tweaking or replanting. Not to mention the variable British weather and the constant battle with nature, including moles, badgers, deer and rabbits.

The year 2015 marks the Gardens' 250th birthday. That is quite an achievement for one family's continued care and devotion from one generation to another. To mark the occasion and to maybe inspire future botanical travellers and gardeners, a 'Burma rope bridge' has been constructed over the bottom pond and through our Jurassic Garden with its giant tree ferns and tropical foliage.

With only a relatively small team of four gardeners and a never-ending list of jobs, we have achieved a lot, creating a garden that changes pace at every

Burma rope bridge constructed in 2015 to celebrate the Gardens' 250th year and enhance the Himalayan and jungle planting.

turn of the path, from open woodland glades to cool and relaxing lawn and herbaceous borders – an endearing atmosphere that brings visitors back year after year. To quote HRH Prince Charles when referring to his own precious garden at Highgrove: 'A good garden feeds the soul, warms the heart and delights the eye'. Hopefully we have nearly achieved this.

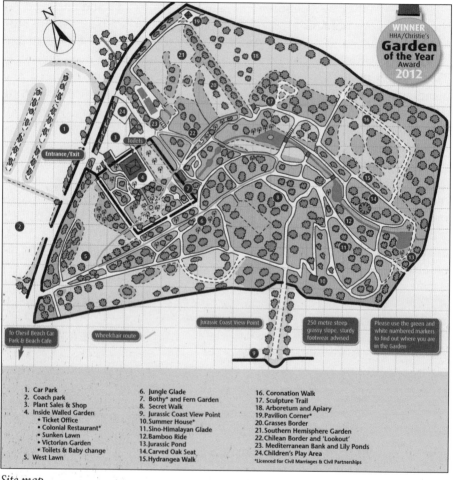

1. Car Park
2. Coach park
3. Plant Sales & Shop
4. Inside Walled Garden
 • Ticket Office
 • Colonial Restaurant*
 • Sunken Lawn
 • Victorian Garden
 • Toilets & Baby change
5. West Lawn
6. Jungle Glade
7. Bothy* and Fern Garden
8. Secret Walk
9. Jurassic Coast View Point
10. Summer House*
11. Sino-Himalayan Glade
12. Bamboo Ride
13. Jurassic Pond
14. Carved Oak Seat
15. Hydrangea Walk
16. Coronation Walk
17. Sculpture Trail
18. Arboretum and Apiary
19. Pavilion Corner*
20. Grasses Border
21. Southern Hemisphere Garden
22. Chilean Border and 'Lookout'
23. Mediterranean Bank and Lily Ponds
24. Children's Play Area
*Licenced for Civil Marriages & Civil Partnerships

Site map

About the Author
Head Gardener
Stephen Griffith

My first job in 1973 was as a Surveyor's Assistant, involving long hours standing holding ranging rods and measuring chains. It was the fact that it was an outdoor job that had attracted me. I moved on to the fruit orchards at Long Ashton Horticultural Research Station near Bristol, where I worked in the plantations section, driving tractors, pruning fruit trees and harvesting apples. With this horticultural experience behind me I went on to Cannington, the Somerset Institute for Horticulture and Agriculture College near Bridgewater. Here I did a 3-year diploma in Amenity Horticulture. This included learning landscape design, nursery plant propagation, botany and arboriculture, with the middle industrial year working for Bristol Parks department.

On leaving college I had a taste for adventure, and found work in the risky business of tree surgery/climbing with Southern Tree Surgeons in Ireland and Germany. In 1980 I made the move into landscaping and plantsmanship. I drove my van down to the South of France and found work on the Cote d'Azur, gardening for private villas and working for a landscape architect on various exclusive properties. In 1982 I successfully applied to work as a Horticultural Landscape Manager on development projects in Saudi Arabia with a Lebanese company, managing vast construction sites and private villas for King Abdulla and his government offices in Riyadh. Later I worked for a company called Arabian Homes creating village complexes for the oil industry in Jeddah and Yanbu. When my 2-year contract ended I travelled through Asia and worked for 6 months in Hong Kong for a 'hydro seeding' company in the New Territories, which was the mainland close to the Chinese border.

On returning to the UK I set up my own landscaping business for a couple of years in north Somerset, but changed course again when an interesting job opportunity came along managing a nursery and butterfly farm on the Isles of Scilly. Later the family who owned it sold the business.

I then worked as Head Gardener for private estate gardens such as the Manor of Cadland in the New Forest, a Capability-Brown landscaped garden on the shores of the Solent, and Sezincote in the Cotswolds. After a couple of years I yearned to be back by the sea, when a rare chance to work on another island as Head Gardener and Estate Manager at La Ville Roussel on Sark in the Channel Islands came along. Island life suited myself and Sara, my wife, my love of fishing, sailing and windsurfing, bird-watching and long coastal walks; however, the job was not very inspirational or demanding and the arrival of our first child meant we had to start thinking about future private schooling and medical costs – there is no National Health Service on Sark.

In 1985 the BBC broadcast an episode of *Gardener's World* from a wild woodland garden, full of Chusan Palms and looking quite different to any other mainland garden I had seen before. It was somewhere close to the famous Dorset Chesil Beach. In 1990 I saw an advert in *Horticulture Week* for a Gardens Manager at Abbotsbury Subtropical Gardens. It was the garden I had seen on TV in 1985 and offered a real management opportunity and greater security for our young family.

After a grilling interview by the Abbotsbury Land Agent, there followed a set of questions and plant identification tests in the Gardens from my old college tutor Roy Cheek, now a horticultural consultant. Another more informal meeting was arranged at Magnolia House on Guernsey, home of Dowager Viscountess Wimborne, who turned out to be the most charming and knowledgeable fellow gardener. She said she had 'always wanted a real gardener for Abbotsbury, it's what the place has lacked for so many years'. She was Great Aunt to Mrs

Townshend, the owner of Abbotsbury Gardens, she was on the board of trustees for the Gardens and affectionately known as Aunt Mabe. The rest is history.

Stephen is a member of the Royal Horticultural Society's Woody Plant Committee, Member of the Institute of Horticulture, and Fellow of the Winston Churchill Memorial Trust. He has regularly appeared in the press and on television for Abbotsbury Gardens. He is an author, artist and photographer. In his capacity as Curator/Head Gardener he is also an experienced horticultural advisor, lecturer and tour guide for botanical holidays, both home and worldwide.

Acknowledgements

Thanks to David Stevens in Abbotsbury for the use of some of his amazing historical postcard collection to help tell the story, of which copyright holders and publishers are no longer in business.

Also for the time-consuming work of Professor Larry Shaaf for making available online the letters of the correspondence of William Henry Fox Talbot, from which so much history has been discovered.

My thanks to Mrs Townshend for her approval to go ahead and write this book and also to Pam Gomer, Mrs Townshend's secretary, who I have constantly been badgering for extra information. Also to Pat Molineux for her diligent work on the Estates' archives and in deciphering old hand-written 19th-century letters. The interim report on historical development for the Gardens by Andy Poore has also been of great importance. Thanks to John Houston of Ilchester Estates for helping implement this publication and to Julie and Tim Musk at Roving Press who have painstakingly edited and reorganised this book to make it a more fluid account and narrative of the Gardens' history. Last but not least, thanks to my wife Sara who put up with my many hours of lock-down at the computer.

A charabanc outing to Abbotsbury from Weymouth.

References and Further Reading

Acland, H. (1993 edn) *The Acland Journal*. Hampshire County Council.

Arnold, H.J.P. (1977) *William Henry Fox Talbot, Pioneer of Photography and Man of Science*. Hutchinson Benham.

Atterbury, P. (2004) *Greetings from Abbotsbury*. Post Card Press.

Boswell, J. and Bailey, M. (1951 edn) *Boswell's Column. Being his Seventy Contributions to The London Magazine (1777–1783)*. William Kimber.

Brunsden, D. (2003) *The Official Guide to the Jurassic Coast*. Coastal Publishing.

Coker, Rev J. (1732) *A Survey of Dorsetshire*. Dorset Publishing Company.

Collins, A. and Brydges, E. (1812) *Collins's Peerage of England; Geneaological, Biographical and Historical*. Kessinger Publishing.

Country Life Illustrated (1899) Abbotsbury Gardens. *The Country Life Illustrated*.

Cruickshanks, E., Handley, S. and Hayton, D.W. (2002) *The House of Commons 1690–1715*. Cambridge University Press.

Earl of Ilchester (1946) *Elizabeth, Lady Holland to her Son 1821–1845*. J. Murray.

Fox Talbot, W.H. (1847) *English Etymologies*. John Murray.

Frampton, M. and Mundy, H.G. (1885) *The Journal of Mary Frampton*. Sampson Low, Marston, Searle and Rivington.

Franklin, R.M. (2005) *Captain Loxley's Little Dog and Lassie the Life Saving Collie*. Diggory Press.

Gardiner, J. (2012) *Magnolias: A Gardener's Guide*. Timber Press.

Geiger, R. (1950) *The Climate Near the Ground*, 2nd edn. Harvard University Press.

Gloag, M.R. (1906) *A Book of English Gardens*. Kessinger Publishing.

Grey, C.H. (1954) *Abbotsbury, A Great Sub-Tropical Garden*. Northern Gardener.

Griffith, S.J. (2003) *Big Leaves for Exotic Effect*. Guild of Master Craftsman Publications.

Harper, C.G. (1905) *The Dorset Coast*. Chapman and Hall.

Harvey, J. (1974) *Early Nurseryman*. Phillimore & Co.

Henning, B.D. (n.d.) *The House of Commons 1660–1690*.

Hutchins, J. (1861–73, 4 vols) *The History and Antiquities of the County of Dorset*. John Bowyer Nichols and Sons.

Jeffery, S. (2004) *Sir Stephen Fox's Extraordinarily Fine Garden at Chiswick*. Garden History Society.

Livingstone, D. (1857) *Missionary Travels and Researches in South Africa*. John Murray.

Martin, J. (1993) *The Penrice Letters 1768–1795*. South Wales Record Society.

Martin, J. (2004) *Wives and Daughters*. Hamilton and London.

Matthew, H.C.C. and Harrison, B. (1995) *Oxford Dictionary of National Biography.* Oxford University Press.

Melville, N. (2006) *Abbotsbury: The Appreciation Revisited* (pp. 38–39). Odun Books.

Millgate, M. (1998) *Thomas Hardy: A Biography.* Clarendon Press.

Poore, A. (1997) *Abbotsbury Gardens: Interim Report on Historical Development.* Ilchester Estates.

Rowson, J.W. (2007 edn) *Bridport and the Great War.* Nigel J Clarke Publications.

St George, Sir H., Lennard, S. and Ryland, J.P. (1885) *The Visitation of the County of Dorset in 1623.* The Harleian Society.

Shaaf, P. L. (n.d.) *The Correspondence of William Fox Talbot.* Retrieved from www.foxtalbot.dmu.ac.uk.

Sheppard, S. (2003) *Seeds of Fortune, A Gardening Dynasty.* Bloomsbury.

The Gardeners Chronicle (n.d.).

The Morning Post (1814, 12 Oct) Royal visit. *The Morning Post.*

The Times (1935, 1 Nov). Mary Lady Ilchester. *The Times.*

Wedgwood Archive (n.d.) *The History of Parliment.* http://www.historyofparliamentonline.org/about/latest-research/wedgwood-archive.

Websites

archaeologydataservice.ac.uk
cracroftspeerage.co.uk
thepeerage.com
foxtalbot.dmu.ac.uk
www.chgt.org.uk
www.jamesboswell.info.

Abbotsbury Through the Seasons

Above: Magnolia Walk in the spring. Below: Ariel picture of tree canopy.

Victorian Garden with spring bedding.

Mediterranean Bank in July.

Melplash Agricultural Show 2013, with David Sutton and Tim Newman.

Cyathea australis 'The Rough Tree Fern' from Australia.

Autumn colour in the Himalayan Glade.

Daffodil bulb planting on Magnolia Walk.

Ginkgo and Maple trees with autumn colour.

Snowfall in the Sunken Lawn.

Hollies and Mahonia provide winter interest.

Gardens shop with seasonal decoration.

Index